Praise for
DEMYSTIFYING C
BUZZWORDS

"Words are powerful. Consider two opening lines: 'In the beginning God created the heavens and the earth,' and 'In the beginning was the Word . . . and the Word was God.' Gary Snodgrass addresses the weight of words—not in a religious or poetic sense but in how business language can shape decisions, behavior, and culture.

I had the privilege of working with Gary for more than forty years. While I focused on legal and executive leadership through major M&A transactions, turnarounds, and leading international businesses, Gary became a recognized expert in HR strategy, organizational and succession planning, and C-suite coaching. His insights and discipline around communication have been sought after globally.

We were shaped early by a boss who insisted we write concisely and with purpose, cutting anything less. Gary never forgot that lesson. This book is his way of sharing that discipline with others: Say more with less, aim for clarity, never confuse verbosity with wisdom, and avoid sowing confusion in your business communications."

—**Michael P. Kane, Esq.,** retired chief executive officer
and managing director

"The lifeblood of leadership and management is effective communication. Corporations' informal vocabulary, short-hand, or slang can jazz up information flow, making it catchy and adding color. But too often our buzzwords become lazy talk—we use phrasing that lacks precision and fuzzes the message. *Demystifying Corporate Buzzwords* pins down how we can immediately reduce ambiguity, tighten our terminology, and lead more powerfully."

—**Price Pritchett, PhD,** CEO, PRITCHETT, LP

"*Demystifying Corporate Buzzwords* is a must-read for business practitioners, communicators, and students of business. Gary Snodgrass demystifies today's corporate jargon and shares tools to communicate masterfully."

—**Ruth Ann Gillis,** independent board director and former Fortune 500 C-suite executive

A PRACTICAL GUIDE TO CLEAR
BUSINESS COMMUNICATION

DEMYSTIFYING
CORPORATE
BUZZWORDS

S. GARY SNODGRASS

RIVER GROVE
BOOKS

Published by River Grove Books
Austin, TX
www.rivergrovebooks.com

Distributed by River Grove Books

Design and composition by Greenleaf Book Group
Cover design by Greenleaf Book Group
Cover images used under license from ©Adobestock.com

Publisher's Cataloging-in-Publication data is available.

Print ISBN: 978-1-966629-75-7

eBook ISBN: 978-1-966629-76-4

First Edition

CONTENTS

ACKNOWLEDGMENTS

THIS BOOK IS DEDICATED TO MY WIFE, Patsy T. Snodgrass—my trusted collaborator, wise adviser, constant supporter, and lifelong partner in every sense.

I am also indebted to my parents, Lloyd and Jerry Snodgrass; to my brother, Steven L. Snodgrass, MD; and to my business colleagues who have provided support and valued partnership, including Jack Skolds, John Samolis, Ginny Brown, Vic Fonseca, Chris Pett, Cathy Costello-Heiron, Carol Kleiman, Al Borm, Greg Puchalski, Bruce Ralph, Brian Cook, Chris Rosenthal, Jeff Rodewald, Margaret Clark, Dr. Hank Tufts, Marilyn B. Tedesco, Robert B. Kerr, Dr. Joel S. Bolante, and many others.

And finally, to my children and their families: Patrick and Amy B. Snodgrass, Amy S. and Parker Fretwell, and Matthew Snodgrass. Special thanks to Amy S. Fretwell for editorial assistance.

NOTE FROM THE AUTHOR

WE'VE ALL SAT IN MEETINGS where someone says we need to "move the needle," "circle back," or "pivot," and we nod along, unsure of what was just said or what to do next. I've been in those rooms. I've led them. Over the years, I began paying attention to the way we use language at work—not just what we say but how those words shape our understanding, behavior, and culture.

This book was born from that curiosity and from a desire to help professionals cut through the fog of corporate jargon without discarding the entire dictionary. I've seen firsthand how well-intentioned words can obscure meaning, cause confusion, or even undermine trust. But I've also seen how the right words, used with clarity and intention, can build alignment, energize teams, and drive results.

Demystifying Corporate Buzzwords: A Practical Guide to Clear Business Communication is not an attack on language; it's a guide for using it more effectively. I trust that you'll leave this book with a sharper ear, a more unmistakable voice, and the tools to communicate with precision and purpose.

Thank you for picking it up.

S. Gary Snodgrass

INTRODUCTION

IN MY MANY YEARS IN CORPORATE BOARDROOMS, I've participated in countless strategy sessions where terms like "move the needle" and "synergy" were frequently used. Executives would inspire their teams with phrases like "think outside the box" or "leverage best practices." These clichés, or buzzwords, often serve as shorthand for complex ideas, making them practical communication tools. They represent how businesses communicate and collaborate. They are intended to inspire, simplify complex concepts, or demonstrate expertise.

But these vague or misaligned terms sometimes left even seasoned professionals like me uncertain of what actions must be taken next. Buzzwords can mask unclear thinking, alienate others, and frustrate teams who crave straight talk. Some people love them, others roll their eyes, but no one can avoid them.

Knowing when and how to use corporate clichés or buzzwords strategically is the key. This book isn't about eliminating buzzwords; it's about making them work for you. Whether you're in a boardroom, on a conference call, or crafting an email, the language you use shapes perceptions, influences decisions, and drives action.

Throughout these chapters, we discuss how to identify the difference between impactful and empty jargon, refine your message for clarity, and harness the correct language to influence and engage. We explore the origins of these buzzwords, their persistence, and the impact they have on workplace communication. We also learn how to use the language more effectively by transforming business vernacular into meaningful dialogue.

A Practical and Engaging Approach

However, knowing the right way to use a word is only part of the challenge. The application of language in the workplace has a direct impact on business decisions, culture, and outcomes. That's why, in addition to defining and analyzing these terms, real-world cases are interwoven throughout the five buzzword sections. This approach enables you to observe how buzzwords are applied in real-world business scenarios, showcasing both effective practices and common pitfalls. These cases range from corporate strategy decisions to leadership challenges and team dynamics, showing when a phrase truly drives action—and when it's just empty talk.

By placing cases within each chapter, you immediately see the relevance of each buzzword in action. For example, in the Strategy and Vision section, we explore how companies have successfully "moved the needle" by shifting focus from short-term gains to long-term value. In Performance and Productivity, we see what happens when teams fail to define "low-hanging fruit," "hit the ground running," and "raise the bar," and how successful leaders turn jargon into real efficiency. By integrating case studies in this way, you gain a more immersive learning experience—one that directly connects the buzzwords to business decision-making.

The case studies highlight the following:

- The consequences of misusing a buzzword—showing how vague, unclear, or careless language can create confusion, stall projects, or lead to strategic missteps.
- How individuals and organizations course-corrected, transforming empty jargon into meaningful, results-driven communication.
- Practical takeaways to ensure you can apply these lessons in your workplace.

How to Use This Book

This book is structured for easy reference and practical application. Each chapter covers a key category of business language:

✓ **Strategy and Vision**—Words that define direction, big-picture thinking, and long-term goals.

✓ **Performance and Productivity**—Buzzwords that impact efficiency, metrics, and results.

✓ **Leadership and Teamwork**—Language that inspires collaboration, motivation, and influence.

✓ **Innovation and Change**—Phrases that drive transformation, agility, and forward-thinking initiatives.

✓ **Communication and Decision-Making**—Terms that shape discussions, align stakeholders, and lead to action.

Each buzzword follows a structured breakdown:

✓ **What It Means**—A clear definition in real business terms.

✓ **How It's Often Misused**—Examples of when the phrase creates confusion or fails to make an impact.

✓ **Actionable Ways to Make It Meaningful**—Practical strategies to utilize the term effectively and ensure it yields actual outcomes.

At the end of each chapter, I have also included brief real-world cases illustrating both practical use and common missteps in applying the terms.

Honorable Mentions Chapter

In addition to the thirty-one thoroughly analyzed buzzwords featured in this book in the categories just described, you will also find a dedicated chapter for Honorable Mentions. This section includes an extra set of frequently used buzzwords that, while prevalent in corporate communication, do not require the same level of in-depth treatment.

Rather than presenting each in a structured format, the Honorable Mentions are shared in a concise, narrative style. Each entry provides a brief reflection on how the phrase is commonly used, where it can go awry, and how to make it more effective. The buzzwords serve as a practical middle ground, offering clarity and context without overwhelming the reader.

To bring balance, voice, and a touch of humor to the conversation, the chapter concludes with a short section titled "Buzzwords with a Wink." These are phrases we've all heard (some we still use), and they reflect the lighter, more colorful side of workplace language. This addition reminds us that while clarity and intention are essential, a touch of levity goes a long way in helping us recognize and refine our communication in professional settings.

The Strategic Buzzword Toolkit: Beyond the Pages

Understanding the concept of buzzwords is just the first step. To truly master them, professionals must practice applying them in real-world situations. That's why this book includes a Strategic Buzzword Toolkit in the Addendum—a hands-on learning section designed to deepen your understanding of when and how to use buzzwords effectively.

The Toolkit features the following:

- ✓ **Interactive Exercises**—Practical activities that challenge you to analyze, reframe, and use buzzwords in meaningful ways.
- ✓ **Assessments**—Self-evaluation tools to help identify patterns in your communication style and pinpoint areas for improvement.
- ✓ **Reflection Points**—Thought-provoking questions to encourage deeper consideration of buzzword usage, ensuring that your language always adds value.

The goal of this section is to help you develop a heightened awareness of the impact of your words, recognizing when a buzzword enhances your message and when it compromises clarity. By completing these exercises, you will improve your ability to communicate with precision, credibility, and authenticity.

Why This Matters

Buzzwords don't have to be meaningless. When used with intention, they can unify teams, clarify objectives, and inspire action. However, when thrown around carelessly, they create ambiguity, disengagement, and even frustration. The key is to recognize when a phrase adds value and when it's just noise.

By the end of this book, you'll be equipped to cut through corporate jargon, communicate with impact, and use business language as a tool for clarity rather than confusion. Whether you're an executive, manager, entrepreneur, or team member, mastering this skill will enhance your credibility, influence, and effectiveness in any business environment.

Let's get started.

1

STRATEGY AND VISION
BUZZWORDS

THESE BUZZWORDS ARE OFTEN USED to communicate high-level thinking and vision. However, they can become empty if they don't support specific actions or measurable goals.

Every business needs a clear strategy and vision. These guiding principles shape decisions, define company direction, and inspire teams. Strategic buzzwords like "big picture" and "game changer" are often used to rally employees and align goals. When used correctly, they help articulate high-level thinking and encourage long-term planning.

However, the problem with strategy-related buzzwords is that they can become overused to the point of meaninglessness. Saying that a project is a "paradigm shift" or a "game changer" does not make it so. Leaders must ensure that actual actions and measurable outcomes support these phrases.

Buzzwords and cases in this chapter include the following:

- Think Big Picture
- Leverage Synergies
- Shift the Paradigm
- Game Changer
- Move the Needle
- Mission Critical
- "The Big Picture Blind Spot" (Comprehensive Case)
- "Moving the Needle . . . or Just Shuffling the Deck?" (Snapshot Case)
- "Mission Critical—and Misaligned" (Snapshot Case)

Think Big Picture

What It Means:

- Taking a broad, strategic view of a situation rather than focusing on minute details.
- Considering long-term goals, overall impact, and interconnected factors in decision-making.

How It's Often Misused:

- Used as a dismissive response to avoid discussing necessary details. (Example: "Don't worry about the specifics—just think big picture.")
- Applied without context, leaving teams unclear about how the "big picture" connects to day-to-day work.

Actionable Ways to Make It Meaningful:

✓ **Provide context**—Instead of just saying "think big picture," explain what the broader vision entails. (Example: "Think big picture—we are positioning ourselves to be the market leaders in sustainable energy over the next five years.")

✓ **Balance macro and micro views**—Encourage teams to connect daily tasks to strategic objectives. (Example: "We need to think big picture—our goal is global expansion, so let's evaluate how this project launch fits into that.")

✓ **Use data-driven insights**—Support broad vision statements with specific metrics or trends.

Leverage Synergies

What It Means:

- Combining strengths, resources, or efforts to achieve results more significant than the sum of individual contributions.
- Common in mergers, partnerships, or cross-functional collaboration, where efficiencies can be maximized.

How It's Often Misused:

- Used as corporate jargon without specifics, making it unclear what synergies are being leveraged. (Example: "We need to leverage synergies across teams" without saying how or why.)

- Applied in situations where no real synergy exists, leading to forced collaboration.

Actionable Ways to Make It Meaningful:

✓ **Clarify what the synergy is**—Instead of saying "Let's leverage synergies," specify what is being combined and why it's valuable. (Example: "By combining our sales and marketing data, we can leverage synergies to target customers more effectively.")

✓ **Quantify the benefit**—Explain how leveraging synergies will lead to efficiency, cost savings, or innovation. (Example: "Merging these two teams will leverage synergies, reducing duplicate work and cutting expenses by 20 percent.")

✓ **Ensure alignment**—Collaboration should make strategic sense and not just be forced for the sake of synergy.

Shift the Paradigm

What It Means:

- A fundamental change in thinking, approach, or business model that redefines how things are done.
- A transformative shift that challenges existing norms, creating new standards or innovative ways of operating.

How It's Often Misused:

- "We're shifting the paradigm," but the company is only making small, incremental changes rather than actual transformations.
- The term "paradigm shift" is often used as a buzzword, but leadership simply repackages old ideas.

Actionable Ways to Make It Meaningful:

- ✓ **Identify and communicate the fundamental shift—** Clearly explain what is changing and how things will operate going forward. (Example: Moving from in-person retail to a fully digital e-commerce mode similar to Amazon.)
- ✓ **Ensure structural or operational change—**Paradigm shifts will be accompanied by significant workplace changes. (Example: Shifting from a hierarchical to a decentralized, team-driven model.)
- ✓ **Back it with a measurable impact—**Quantify the paradigm shift as critical to the business. (Example: A company adopting AI-driven customer service reduces response times by 50 percent and increases customer satisfaction scores by 20 percent.)

Game Changer

What It Means:

- A strategy, innovation, or event that fundamentally transforms an industry, company, or market.
- It introduces a significant competitive advantage or disrupts the market.

How It's Often Misused:

- Overused to describe small or incremental improvements. (Example: "This software update is a game changer" when it's just a minor feature update.)
- Used without evidence to support the claim.

Actionable Ways to Make It Meaningful:

✓ **Define what makes it a game changer**—Specify why it fundamentally alters the landscape. (Example: "Our AI-driven automation eliminates 80 percent of manual processing—this is a game changer for customer service efficiency.")

✓ **Compare with industry standards**—Show how it sets a new benchmark rather than just another improvement. (Example: "Unlike traditional models, our new product reduces emissions by 90 percent, making it a true game changer.")

✓ **Use it sparingly**—Reserve it for fundamental transformations, not just any new initiative.

Move the Needle

What It Means:

- Making a measurable impact on key performance indicators (KPIs) or business goals.
- Driving significant, noticeable progress rather than small or inconsequential changes.

How It's Often Misused:

- Used as a vague motivational phrase without defining what needs to be moved or by how much. (Example: "We need to move the needle on customer satisfaction" without specifying targets.)
- Applied to small or unclear initiatives that don't create a meaningful difference.

Actionable Ways to Make It Meaningful:

- ✓ **Set measurable goals**—Define what moving the needle looks like. (Example: "To move the needle on revenue, we need to increase monthly sales by at least 15 percent.")

- ✓ **Tie it to business impact**—Show how the action contributes to the overall objectives. (Example: "This new onboarding process will move the needle on employee retention, reducing turnover by 20 percent.")

- ✓ **Use it in data-driven discussions**—Connect the phrase to objective performance metrics rather than using it as a generic directive.

Mission Critical

What It Means:

- A task, process, or initiative that is essential to success—if it fails, the business or project is significantly impacted.
- Often used in IT, security, health care, and business continuity planning, where failure leads to severe consequences.

How It's Often Misused:

- Often applied to everything, making it lose its urgency. (Example: Calling every project "mission critical" when some are of lower priority.)

- Used without clear justification for why something is truly essential.

Actionable Ways to Make It Meaningful:

✓ **Clarify why it's mission critical**—Explain the impact of failure. (Example: "This cybersecurity update is mission critical because a breach could cost us millions and damage customer trust.")

✓ **Prioritize accordingly**—Reserve the term for initiatives that genuinely impact business survival or key strategic goals. (Example: "Launching this product on time is mission critical for securing our market leadership position.")

✓ **Avoid diluting its importance**—Use it sparingly so that when something is mission critical, teams take it seriously.

Strategy and Vision Comprehensive Case Study: "The Big Picture Blind Spot"

Scenario

At BrightEdge Consulting, a midsize firm known for innovative digital marketing strategies, the executive team launched a company-wide initiative called Vision 2028. Its goal: to position the firm as a "game changer" in the analytics and AI-driven branding space. Leadership urged teams to "think big picture" and align their work with long-term transformation. The bold strategy—encompassing global expansion, new AI-based service lines, and a brand overhaul—was all part of the vision.

In leadership meetings, "big picture" was the new mantra. Tactical issues and local operational concerns were routinely sidelined in favor of broader discussions about vision, positioning, and long-term growth. Managers across departments echoed the phrase—sometimes to justify vague plans, other times to avoid confronting near-term challenges.

What Went Wrong?

Despite the grand vision, cracks quickly appeared.

- **Disconnected operations**—Regional offices struggled to meet basic client delivery expectations. Hiring gaps, outdated tools, and process breakdowns were reported but flagged as "details we'll sort out later."

- **Demoralized teams**—Employees on the front lines felt unheard. When they raised concerns, they were told to "think big picture," which became shorthand for "don't bring us problems." Morale declined, and turnover spiked.
- **Vision with no ground game**—The phrase "game changer" was used in internal presentations, sales pitches, and recruiting. Still, there was no clearly defined innovation, product, or differentiator to support it.

Without addressing foundational issues, the big-picture thinking felt hollow. Clients noticed service delays and inconsistent results, and a significant account chose not to renew its contract.

How Was It Fixed?

Facing internal frustration and external reputational risk, BrightEdge's chief operations officer (COO) initiated a strategic recalibration. The goal wasn't to abandon the vision, but rather to reconnect it to reality.

✓ **Reframed the "big picture" as a two-way view**— Leaders created a new approach that balanced strategic thinking with operational listening. Quarterly "reality checks" were instituted to surface local challenges that might threaten long-term goals.

✓ **Defined what "game changer" meant**—Instead of using the term loosely, the leadership team identified two apparent innovations they were investing in: a proprietary AI tool for campaign optimization and a new client transparency dashboard. These became tangible anchors for the company's transformative messaging.

✓ **Aligned internal comms**—Messaging was revised to acknowledge the effort behind the transformation. Internal town halls shifted tone from aspirational only to inclusive and practical, reinforcing that every role mattered in building the big picture.

As a result, team trust improved, and the firm delivered its first real "game changer" six months later—an award-winning client analytics engine that drove measurable results.

Lesson Learned

Big-picture thinking is essential, but it must also encompass the perspective from the ground up. When used without connection to operational realities, it becomes rhetorical. Calling something a "game changer" doesn't make it one—real innovation requires a clear definition and visible execution. Vision only works when people at every level can see where they fit and believe their efforts are part of something real.

Strategy and Vision Snapshot Cases

"Moving the Needle . . . or Just Shuffling the Deck?"

At a national retail chain, the executive team launched a new customer engagement strategy, touting it as a way to really "move the needle" on loyalty and repeat business. The initiative included minor updates to the mobile app, tweaks to loyalty program emails, and a refreshed color palette for in-store signage. Internal presentations were confident, and leadership declared the changes would deliver measurable results in ninety days.

However, when the quarterly reports arrived, customer retention numbers remained flat. Store managers noted that customer behavior hadn't changed, and frontline employees struggled to explain what was different. Behind closed doors, team members admitted that they had focused on surface-level improvements because they were faster and safer than more profound, more comprehensive operational changes.

In the end, to "move the needle," the effort must be meaningful. Cosmetic or low-impact changes rarely produce significant outcomes. Impact requires depth, not just action. Leaders should define what change looks like—and whether the needle was worth moving in the first place.

"Mission Critical—and Misaligned"

At a midsize pharmaceutical company, the product development team was tasked with updating internal compliance documentation to meet new federal guidelines. The project lead framed the initiative as "mission critical," emphasizing the legal and reputational risks associated with not meeting the standards. The phrase triggered immediate escalation—IT redirected resources to support the team, and Marketing paused other campaigns to avoid distraction.

However, as the project progressed, it became apparent that the "mission critical" label wasn't consistently applied across departments. Legal had already completed a compliance review months earlier, and most of the updates were procedural rather than urgent. The inflated label led to resource conflicts and created tension with teams who had to delay their own genuinely time-sensitive work.

When a separate drug launch encountered an unexpected snag, there were insufficient resources available to respond quickly; many were still tied up on the wrongly prioritized "critical" documentation project.

The company learned that "mission critical" must be aligned across the organization. When urgency is overstated, it creates friction rather than focus. Overusing high-stakes language misguides resource allocation. True priorities deserve support—but only if they're justified.

Strategy and Vision Buzzwords Summary

Strategy and vision buzzwords are used to communicate high-level thinking and vision, but they must be accompanied by specifics. Reference the following list when you need a reminder.

- **Think Big Picture**—Think big but connect the dots on the ground.

- **Leverage Synergies**—Identify where strengths overlap and make them work together.

- **Shift the Paradigm**—New outcomes require new mindsets.

- **Game Changer**—It's only a game changer if it changes the game.

- **Move the Needle**—Progress is earned, not assumed. Focus on high-impact change.

- **Mission Critical**—If everything is critical, nothing is. Prioritize what's essential for success.

2

PERFORMANCE AND PRODUCTIVITY BUZZWORDS

THESE BUZZWORDS ARE MEANT to drive action but often lack specificity, making it unclear what should be done.

Every company values productivity, efficiency, and results. Terms like "low-hanging fruit," "streamline," and "optimize" are used to encourage teams to work smarter and faster. When applied correctly, these words can help focus efforts on high-impact tasks and promote more effective resource utilization.

However, productivity buzzwords are often misused to create unrealistic expectations. For example, saying "Let's optimize this process" without defining how or what success looks like can frustrate teams. Calling something "low-hanging fruit" can falsely suggest it's easy, though it may need significant effort.

Buzzwords and cases in this chapter include the following:

- Low-Hanging Fruit
- Burning the Midnight Oil
- Hit the Ground Running
- Raise the Bar
- Streamline
- Best Practices
- Optimize
- "Running Fast, Falling Short" (Comprehensive Case)
- "Stuck Picking Low-Hanging Fruit" (Snapshot Case)
- "Optimizing in All the Wrong Places" (Snapshot Case)

Low-Hanging Fruit

What It Means:

- Easy-to-accomplish tasks or opportunities that require minimal effort but deliver quick benefits.
- Often refers to small, high-impact wins that can be executed immediately.

How It's Often Misused:

- Overused to the point where it diminishes the effort required. (Example: "This is just low-hanging fruit" when it takes significant work.)
- Applied to tasks that are not easy or don't have a high impact, creating unrealistic expectations.

Actionable Ways to Make It Meaningful:

✓ **Clearly define what is low-hanging fruit**—Identify tasks that are quick to execute and deliver immediate value. (Example: "Sending follow-up emails to warm leads is low-hanging fruit that could increase conversions soon.")

✓ **Use it for prioritization**—Help teams focus on quick wins that contribute to significant goals. (Example: A sales team identifies warm leads from past customers as "low-hanging fruit" because they are more likely to convert quickly, allowing the team to focus on them before pursuing new prospects, who require more nurturing.)

✓ **Differentiate from strategic priorities**—Avoid labeling critical or complex tasks as low-hanging fruit. (Example: A tech company might consider fixing minor website bugs as low-hanging fruit since they require minimal effort, whereas developing a new AI-driven feature is a long-term strategic priority that requires significant investment and planning.)

Burning the Midnight Oil

What It Means:

- Working late into the night to complete tasks, often to meet deadlines.
- Implies dedication and hard work, but often at the cost of personal time and well-being.

How It's Often Misused:

- Glorified as a sign of commitment, leading to burnout culture. (Example: "We need to be burning the midnight oil to get this project done" when better planning could prevent overwork.)
- Used to pressure teams into unsustainable workloads rather than fostering efficiency.

Actionable Ways to Make It Meaningful:

✓ **Acknowledge the sacrifice**—If employees are working late, recognize their effort and provide support. (Example: "I appreciate everyone burning the midnight oil, but let's work on a sustainable schedule moving forward.")

✓ **Encourage efficiency over exhaustion**—Prioritize productivity during working hours rather than relying on excessive overtime. (Example: Instead of praising employees for staying late, implement time-blocking techniques and automation tools to help teams complete their work during regular hours.)

✓ **Promote work-life balance**—Instead of praising late-night work, streamline processes to reduce the need for it. (Example: A manager notices an employee frequently working late hours and offers flexible scheduling to ensure employees are not overwhelmed, reinforcing a culture where productivity is valued over excessive hours.)

Hit the Ground Running

What It Means:

- Starting a new project, role, or initiative with immediate momentum and effectiveness.
- Being prepared and proactive from day one.

How It's Often Misused:

- Used without providing proper onboarding. (Example: "We need new hires to hit the ground running" without giving them training or resources.)
- Implies unrealistic expectations for immediate high performance.

Actionable Ways to Make It Meaningful:

✓ **Set up people for success**—Provide resources, training, and clear objectives so they can truly hit the ground running. (Example: "Let's create a structured onboarding plan to help them hit the ground running.")

✓ **Use it when there is preparation**—Ensure the team is ready before launching a new initiative. (Example: A company launching a new software product ensures that the sales team is fully trained, marketing materials are ready, and customer support is equipped with FAQs before the official launch, allowing the team to "hit the ground running" on day one.)

✓ **Balance speed with quality**—Rushing without a solid plan can lead to mistakes and inefficiencies. (Example: A new employee is expected to contribute quickly, but instead of being thrown into projects without guidance, they receive a structured onboarding program and a mentor.)

Raise the Bar

What It Means:

- Setting higher expectations or performance standards to achieve better results.
- Encouraging continuous improvement and excellence.

How It's Often Misused:

- Used without clear benchmarks, making it vague or motivational without action. (Example: "We need to raise the bar" without defining how.)
- Implies continuous escalation without acknowledging realistic goals and progress.

Actionable Ways to Make It Meaningful:

✓ **Define specific goals**—Instead of saying "Raise the bar," set measurable improvement targets. (Example: "We're raising the bar by increasing customer satisfaction scores from 85 percent to 90 percent this quarter.")

✓ **Make it achievable**—Balance ambition with realistic expectations and support. (Example: A company desires to improve customer service response times. Instead of setting unrealistic goals like reducing wait times from ten minutes to one minute overnight, it uses a phased approach to gradually improve results.)

✓ **Recognize progress**—Acknowledge milestones and improvements along the way. (Example: Instead of waiting until a final goal is achieved, acknowledge milestones to keep motivation high.)

Streamline

What It Means:

- Making processes more efficient by reducing complexity, waste, or redundancies.
- Improving workflows to save time, resources, and effort.

How It's Often Misused:

- Used as a vague directive without specifying what is being streamlined. (Example: "We need to streamline operations" without explaining how.)
- Implies cutting corners rather than making thoughtful improvements.

Actionable Ways to Make It Meaningful:

✓ **Identify specific inefficiencies**—Don't be vague. (Example: Instead of saying "Let's streamline our meetings," say "We will reduce meeting frequency and use shared docs for updates.")

✓ **Use technology or automation**—Find ways to eliminate manual tasks where possible. (Example: A company streamlines its invoicing process by implementing automated billing software, reducing manual data errors and cutting processing time from two days to just a few hours.)

✓ **Ensure quality is maintained**—Streamlining should improve efficiency without sacrificing accuracy or customer experience. (Example: A manufacturing company eliminates unnecessary production steps to speed up output, but before implementation, it conducts quality control testing to ensure performance is not compromised.)

Best Practices

What It Means:

- Proven, effective methods used by top performers in an industry.
- Strategies that lead to success and efficiency based upon experience and research.

How It's Often Misused:

- Used without adaptation to fit a company's unique context. (Example: "Let's implement industry best practices" without assessing if they apply.)
- Overapplied as a buzzword without clear action steps.

Actionable Ways to Make It Meaningful:

✓ **Customize for your business**—Instead of simply following industry norms, evaluate which best practices fit your company's goals and culture. (Example: A retail company adopts an inventory management best practice from the tech industry but modifies it to fit their unique business model.)

✓ **Back it with data**—Support best practices with case studies, research, or performance metrics. (Example: Instead of unthinkingly following an industry best practice for posting on social media three times a day, the company researched their audience and learned that their customers respond better to five high-quality posts per week rather than frequent, lower-impact posts.)

✓ **Evolve best practices over time**—What worked in the past may need updating. (Example: "We'll implement best practices from GE but based upon our specific customer needs.")

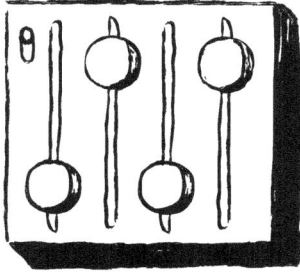

Optimize

What It Means:

- Improving a process, system, or strategy to make it as effective as possible.
- Finding ways to increase efficiency, performance, or results.

How It's Often Misused:

- Used without clear direction, making it meaningless. (Example: "We need to optimize our marketing" without specifying what aspect.)
- Implies endless tweaking instead of strategic improvement.

Actionable Ways to Make It Meaningful:

✓ **Define what's being optimized**—Give more than a general statement. (Example: "We're optimizing our website speed by reducing load time from five seconds to two seconds.")

✓ **Use metrics to track improvement**—Optimization should be measurable. (Example: "We optimized our email campaigns, increasing open rates from 20 percent to 30 percent.")

✓ **Prioritize key areas**—Focus on high-impact areas rather than trying to optimize everything at once. (Example: A manufacturing plant wants to optimize efficiency, but instead of overhauling everything at once, they first focus on reducing material waste in production, since it has the biggest cost impact, before moving on to other improvements.)

Performance and Productivity Comprehensive Case Study: "Running Fast, Falling Short"

Scenario

Velocity Systems, a midsize software company, had just acquired a smaller AI start-up to accelerate development on its next-generation analytics platform. To demonstrate momentum to investors and the board, senior leadership promised that the newly combined team would "hit the ground running" with a product beta release in just ninety days.

The integration team received clear marching orders: no delays, no onboarding buffer, and no need to slow down due to growing pains. Project managers were also informed that this would be an opportunity to "raise the bar" on performance, demonstrating that the company could operate with start-up speed while scaling up.

There was a kickoff event, high-energy messaging, and optimistic deadlines—but no real alignment between teams, tools, or expectations.

What Went Wrong?

By prioritizing speed and aspiration over structure and clarity, leadership misread the situation.

- **Premature acceleration**—The new team hadn't even gained access to the company's core codebase, documentation standards, or internal tools before being assigned major deliverables. Early sprints were chaotic, and quality suffered.

- **Undefined standards**—The phrase "raise the bar" was used frequently, but no one defined what success looked like. Employees interpreted it differently—some focused on faster turnaround while others assumed it meant new feature innovation. The lack of clarity led to missed expectations on all sides.

- **Frustrated talent**—The acquired team felt undervalued. Many left stable roles to join the new venture, only to be thrown into a high-pressure environment with little guidance or context. Several top developers requested transfers or left within weeks.

- **Optics over outcomes**—Leadership reported to the board that the integration was "on track," but internally, trust was slipping and real progress stalled.

How Was It Fixed?

After an anonymous employee pulse survey revealed burnout and confusion, the COO stepped in with a reboot plan.

- ✓ **Redefined "hitting the ground running"**—Rather than diving in without thinking, the company built a three-week onboarding sprint for all incoming teams, with tools, mentors, and a road map. Speed was still a goal, but so was informed engagement.

- ✓ **Clarified "raise the bar"**—Leaders worked with team leads to define specific stretch goals tied to quality, innovation, and collaboration, not just speed. These became visible benchmarks for progress.

✓ **Rebuilt team trust**—Managers held retrospective sessions to acknowledge the missteps and invite feedback on how to move forward more sustainably. Transparency helped regain confidence.

✓ **Shifted focus to long-term health**—Leadership realigned performance reviews to reward thoughtful contributions, not just output volume. By doing so, they built a healthier and more effective pace of work.

Lesson Learned

Speed without structure is risk, not readiness. Saying a team should "hit the ground running" sounds bold, but without proper orientation, it can lead to missteps. And telling teams to "raise the bar" without defining what that means invites confusion, not excellence.

If you want to move fast and raise standards, prepare people, align expectations, and define success. That's how momentum becomes progress and pressure becomes performance.

Performance and Productivity Snapshot Cases

"Stuck Picking Low-Hanging Fruit"

At a midsize financial services firm, the operations team launched a workflow improvement campaign with the goal of increasing internal efficiency. In early meetings, the department lead urged everyone to focus on "low-hanging fruit"—quick fixes and easy wins that could be implemented immediately. The team responded quickly: They removed duplicated forms, shortened some approval chains, and updated shared templates. Metrics improved slightly, and leadership praised the momentum.

But as the initiative continued, the team remained in "quick fix" mode, even when more impactful—but complex—issues were clearly visible. Efforts to revamp the outdated client onboarding system or reduce delays in compliance reviews were dismissed as "too big for now." Six months later, the project stalled. Frontline staff grew frustrated that more profound challenges were being ignored, and leadership realized that incrementalism had become a ceiling.

The company learned that quick wins matter—but they're not a strategy. Use low-hanging fruit to build momentum, not to avoid real change. Don't stop climbing. If you never venture beyond what's easy, you won't achieve what's necessary.

"Optimizing in All the Wrong Places"

A national apparel brand sought to "optimize" its supply chain to enhance cost efficiency and reduce time to market. Consultants recommended several AI-based tools to "streamline" inventory tracking and vendor communication. Within two months, the company rolled out new systems, before fully training staff or aligning the tools with their seasonal order patterns.

The software worked perfectly on paper, but in practice, warehouse teams were overwhelmed, delays increased, and several shipments missed retail delivery windows. The company had "optimized" a process it didn't fully understand and, in doing so, made it worse. After a rocky quarter, they paused the rollout of automation. They returned to basics—interviewing frontline employees, reviewing order patterns, and building a hybrid solution that actually fit how the business operated.

The company learned that optimization without insight is just disruption. Efficiency requires understanding the system, not just upgrading it. Also, technology isn't a shortcut. Tools work best when built around people, not the other way around.

Performance and Productivity Buzzwords Summary

Performance and productivity buzzwords can drive action, but they should be supported by clear, actionable steps. Reference the following list when you need a reminder.

- **Low-Hanging Fruit**—Quick wins that drive immediate impact.
- **Burning the Midnight Oil**—Sustained effort should not replace smart efficiency.
- **Hit the Ground Running**—Preparation enables rapid and effective execution.

- **Raise the Bar**—Set higher standards with clear, measurable goals.
- **Streamline**—Improve processes without sacrificing quality or performance.
- **Best Practices**—Proven methods should evolve with innovation.
- **Optimize**—Refine processes for maximum efficiency and impact.

3

LEADERSHIP AND TEAMWORK BUZZWORDS

STRONG LEADERSHIP AND EFFECTIVE TEAMWORK ARE critical to any organization. Buzzwords like "empower," "alignment," and "win-win" are meant to foster collaboration and inspire teams. Effective leaders utilize these terms to promote shared goals and motivate their employees.

However, leadership jargon is often used as a substitute for authentic engagement. "Let's align on this," without clear communication, can lead to misunderstandings. Telling employees that they are "empowered" without providing them with actual authority or resources can create frustration.

Buzzwords and cases in this chapter include the following:

- Empower
- Take It Offline

- Alignment
- Circle Back
- Win-Win
- Thought Leadership
- "Empowering Without Alignment" (Comprehensive Case)
- "Let's Circle Back on That" (Snapshot Case)
- "A Real Win-Win That Wasn't" (Snapshot Case)

Empower

What It Means:

- Giving people the authority, resources, and confidence to take initiative and make decisions.
- Encouraging autonomy and responsibility rather than micromanaging.

How It's Often Misused:

- Used as a vague motivational term without actual action. (Example: "We need to empower employees" without changing policies or processes to support them.)

- Sometimes used to shift responsibility without support. (Example: "You're empowered to handle this" but the person lacks training or authority.)

Actionable Ways to Make It Meaningful:

✓ **Provide clear authority and resources**—Instead of just saying "We empower our team," give employees decision-making power. (Example: "You have full authority to approve customer discounts up to 10 percent without manager approval.")

✓ **Encourage skill development**—Empowerment should include training and mentorship to ensure confidence in decision-making.

✓ **Create accountability, not burden**—Empowerment means trusting employees, not just passing off difficult tasks. (Example: "We empower our team to lead projects and provide guidance when needed.")

Take It Offline

What It Means:

- Moving a discussion from a group setting or meeting to a one-on-one or smaller follow-up conversation.
- Avoiding derailing a discussion or diving too deep into details in a broader setting.

How It's Often Misused:

- Used to avoid difficult conversations rather than address them. (Example: "Let's take this offline" without ever actually following up.)
- Misused by pushing aside important discussions when they need immediate attention.

Actionable Ways to Make It Meaningful:

✓ **Follow through with action**—If you say "Let's take this offline," make sure to set a time to discuss it. (Example: "Let's take this offline—I'll schedule a follow-up this afternoon.")

✓ **Use it when necessary, not to avoid transparency—** Some discussions should happen in the group setting rather than be sidelined.

✓ **Clarify the purpose**—Instead of vaguely saying "We'll take this offline," say why. (Example: "Let's take this offline so we can review the data in detail.")

Alignment

What It Means:

- Ensuring that teams, departments, or individuals are working toward the same goals.
- Creating consistency in strategy, messaging, and execution.

How It's Often Misused:

- Used without specificity, making it unclear what needs to align. (Example: "We need alignment across teams" without defining areas for improvement.)
- Sometimes misused to force agreement, even when different perspectives are valuable.

Actionable Ways to Make It Meaningful:

- ✓ **Clarify what needs alignment**—Instead of just saying "We need alignment," define what specifically needs alignment. (Example: "We need alignment on our product road map before launching.")

- ✓ **Encourage collaboration, not just compliance**—True alignment means ensuring everyone understands the goal and isn't just following orders.

- ✓ **Use data to guide alignment**—If there's misalignment, use metrics or goals to bring teams together. (Example: "Sales and Marketing need alignment on lead conversion goals to ensure consistency.")

Circle Back

What It Means:

- Revisiting a topic, issue, or decision later when more information is available or when the timing is better.
- Ensuring that nothing is left unresolved and that it will be addressed in the future.

How It's Often Misused:

- Used to dismiss issues rather than actually following up. (Example: "Let's circle back on that" with no plan to do so.)
- Creates frustration when it becomes a stalling tactic instead of leading to action.

Actionable Ways to Make It Meaningful:

- ✓ **Set a timeline for circling back**—Instead of vaguely saying "Let's circle back," set a deadline. (Example: "Let's circle back on this next Wednesday after we review the data.")

- ✓ **Ensure follow-through by turning intent into action**—If you promise to revisit an issue, actually do it and document steps and actions taken.

- ✓ **Use it when appropriate, not to avoid decisions**—Don't allow it to become a stalling tactic. Some issues require immediate attention rather than continuous delays.

Win-Win

What It Means:

- Creating a situation where both parties benefit from an agreement or outcome.
- Finding a resolution that balances different interests while creating mutual value.

How It's Often Misused:

- Used to oversimplify complex negotiations, implying that everyone can win when trade-offs are inevitable. It can create false expectations.
- Sometimes applied to one-sided deals where one party benefits significantly more. (Example: "This is a win-win" when it clearly favors or benefits only one side.)

Actionable Ways to Make It Meaningful:

✓ **Clarify how both sides benefit**—Instead of saying "This is a win-win," explain the specific advantages for each party. (Example: "This is a win-win because our partnership reduces costs for you and expands our market reach.")

✓ **Negotiate fairly**—A true win-win considers the needs of both sides and doesn't disguise a one-sided advantage. (Example: Offering flexibility on timelines in exchange for pricing concessions shows mutual give-and-take, not just surface-level agreement.)

✓ **Ensure transparency**—Make sure both parties understand how they're benefiting so the agreement feels genuinely fair. (Example: In a partnership agreement, openly sharing how revenue will be split and how each party's contributions are valued helps build trust and long-term commitment.)

Thought Leadership

What It Means:

- Establishing oneself or an organization as an expert and influencer in an industry by providing valuable insights, innovation, and expertise.
- Creating high-quality content, research, and discussions that shape industry conversations.

How It's Often Misused:

- Used too broadly, making it seem like anyone sharing opinions is a thought leader. (Example: Posting on LinkedIn doesn't make someone a thought leader—it requires expertise and influence.)

- Sometimes used for self-promotion rather than genuine industry contribution.

Actionable Ways to Make It Meaningful:

✓ **Provide original insights, not just opinions**—Thought leadership requires expertise, research, and innovation, not just frequent posting. (Example: "Publishing a research-backed white paper positions our company as a thought leader in AI ethics.")

✓ **Engage in meaningful industry conversations**—Instead of just promoting products, contribute valuable discussions, data, and case studies that inform and elevate the dialogue.

✓ **Demonstrate expertise with consistency**—Thought leadership isn't a one-time action; it requires ongoing contributions to industry advancements. Build credibility over time.

Leadership and Teamwork Comprehensive Case Study: "Empowering Without Alignment"

Scenario

HorizonEdge, a management consulting firm, launched a company-wide initiative called Empower 360 to decentralize decision-making and promote employee-led innovation. The leadership team introduced new team structures and granted greater autonomy to junior staff in client-facing roles. The initiative was introduced with enthusiasm and framed as a move to "empower our people to lead from where they are."

At the same time, the company was revisiting its strategic priorities and client segmentation. However, little was done to ensure the Empower 360 initiative aligned with the evolving business strategy, operational processes, or client expectations.

What Went Wrong?

Despite strong internal messaging around empowerment, confusion quickly emerged.

- **Disjointed decisions**—Client teams began making decisions that contradicted broader company priorities or conflicted with each other. (Example: One junior team decided to offer free diagnostic services to attract new clients, but this directly undercut the firm's premium positioning strategy and created tension with the marketing and pricing teams.)

- **Lack of team cohesion**—The leadership team began noticing miscommunication, duplicated efforts, and inconsistent service delivery.
- **Lack of strategy**—Employees weren't given a shared framework or clear strategic guardrails, making empowerment feel directionless.

Frustrated by the missteps, executives began walking back the initiative, and the phrase "empowerment" became hollow and even sarcastically referenced in meetings. The core issue wasn't the concept of empowerment—it was the lack of alignment.

How Was It Fixed?

HorizonEdge paused Empower 360 and launched a rapid internal review. The leadership team acknowledged that the initiative had been launched without cross-functional alignment or operational clarity. The revised strategy involved three key steps.

- ✓ **Clarified strategic intent**—Empowerment was redefined in the context of the firm's client positioning and goals.
- ✓ **Structured autonomy**—Teams were given freedom to make decisions within clearly defined boundaries linked to KPIs, client priorities, and team roles.

✓ **Reinforced alignment mechanisms**—Regular check-ins, shared dashboards, and cross-functional forums ensured that empowered decisions continued to support the company's strategy.

With greater alignment in place, the firm relaunched the initiative under the name Empower 360 v2, this time embedding alignment into every stage of planning, communication, and execution.

Lesson Learned

Empowerment is only meaningful when it's guided by shared purpose. Without alignment, it can lead to well-intentioned chaos, eroding trust and performance. To empower effectively, leaders must pair autonomy with strategic clarity and ensure that decision-making authority operates within well-communicated boundaries. True empowerment requires clarity of purpose, shared goals, and a sense of structured autonomy.

Leadership and Teamwork Snapshot Cases

"Let's Circle Back on That"

This is the story of when delay becomes avoidance. During a cross-functional product strategy meeting at a midsize tech company, a heated discussion arose regarding the timeline for launching a new customer-facing feature. When a junior analyst raised a concern about unresolved backend integration issues, the VP of product quickly interjected: "Let's circle back on that—we're short on time. We'll take it offline."

The phrases "circle back" and "take it offline" were used, not to manage time effectively but to avoid addressing a valid concern. No follow-up discussion occurred, and the issue resurfaced weeks later—this time as a production delay that cost the company thousands of dollars in customer service and development rework.

Buzzwords intended to defer discussions should not become evasive maneuvers. Taking an issue "offline" should be followed by concrete steps and accountability. "Circle back" must come with ownership and a timeline—or it becomes code for never.

"A Real Win-Win That Wasn't"

It's easy for thought leadership to get lost in the pitch. For example, a B2B marketing agency pitched a new service model to a long-term client, describing it as a "win-win" that would position both companies as thought leaders in their respective industries. The proposal included bundled pricing and joint content development; however, the details heavily favored the agency's internal KPIs over the client's actual objectives.

"Win-win" was used as a rhetorical device to push through an imbalanced proposal. "Thought leadership" was mentioned as a selling point without a clear strategy, defined audience, or measurable impact.

For a true win-win, both parties must benefit and understand how. Thought leadership must be grounded in expertise, relevance, and audience value, rather than being included solely for optics.

Leadership and Teamwork Buzzwords Summary

Leadership and teamwork buzzwords are used to foster collaboration, promote shared goals, and motivate teams. Leadership buzzwords should be backed by real action. Reference the following list when you need a reminder.

- **Empower**—Give real authority and resources, not just words.
- **Take It Offline**—Ensure follow-up, not avoidance.
- **Alignment**—Specify what needs alignment and ensure collaboration.
- **Circle Back**—Follow through with real deadlines, not delays.
- **Win-Win**—Ensure both sides genuinely benefit.
- **Thought Leadership**—Provide real expertise, research, and influence, not just content.

4

INNOVATION AND CHANGE BUZZWORDS

THESE INNOVATION AND CHANGE BUZZWORDS can create confusion instead of progress. The correct terms should inspire action, not just conversation.

Innovation and adaptability are crucial in today's rapidly evolving business landscape. Leaders often say "Think outside the box," but creativity can become unfocused without clear direction. "Blue sky thinking" encourages limitless ideas but must be paired with practical execution.

To be effective, these buzzwords need clarity, intent, and follow-through. They drive real progress rather than just sounding impressive when backed by action.

Buzzwords and cases in this chapter include the following:

- Think Outside the Box
- Blue Sky Thinking
- Change Management
- Growth Mindset
- Breakthrough
- Scalability
- "Too Much Sky, Not Enough Runway" (Comprehensive Case)
- "Thinking Outside the Box—with No Map Back" (Snapshot Case)
- "Scaling Before the Foundation Set" (Snapshot Case)

Think Outside the Box

What It Means:

- Encouraging creativity and unconventional problem-solving instead of sticking to traditional methods.
- Challenging assumptions and limitations to find innovative approaches.

How It's Often Misused:

- Used without clear direction, making it an empty directive. (Example: "Let's think outside the box" without defining what kind of innovation is needed.)
- Often applied to every situation, even when traditional methods are more effective.

Actionable Ways to Make It Meaningful:

✓ **Define what "outside the box" means for the situation**—Instead of just saying "Think outside the box," guide the discussion. (Example: "Let's explore nontraditional sales strategies like AI-driven lead generation.")

✓ **Encourage structured brainstorming**—Innovation works best with a clear framework, rather than just open-ended thinking, to channel creativity into actionable ideas.

✓ **Support risk-taking**—If teams are asked to think creatively, they should feel safe to propose bold ideas without fear of failure. Psychological safety fuels innovation.

Blue Sky Thinking

What It Means:

- Creative, limitless brainstorming that explores bold, unconventional ideas without immediate concern for feasibility.
- Encourages radical innovation and future-focused vision.

How It's Often Misused:

- Used as a filler phrase without real intent. (Example: "Let's do some blue sky thinking" without any real encouragement for bold ideas.)

- Misinterpreted as unrealistic daydreaming rather than structured innovation. (Example: Suggesting a radical shift in business model without a road map can seem impractical unless it's grounded in research and strategic intent.)

Actionable Ways to Make It Meaningful:

- ✓ **Create an environment for bold ideas**—Instead of just saying "Let's do blue sky thinking," set clear innovation goals. (Example: "If there were no budget limits, what new products would we develop?")
- ✓ **Encourage divergent and convergent thinking**—First, generate wild ideas freely, then narrow them down to actionable ones. (Example: A team might brainstorm dozens of unconventional product features, then collaboratively select the top three to prototype and test.)
- ✓ **Tie it back to strategy**—After brainstorming, evaluate ideas based on feasibility and impact. (Example: After a creative session, rank proposals by how well they align with core business goals and available resources.)

Change Management

What It Means:

- Transitioning individuals, teams, and organizations from a current state to a desired future or aspirational state.
- Reducing resistance and improving adoption of new processes, technologies, or company-wide shifts.

How It's Often Misused:

- Announcing changes without involving employees, assuming that just by calling it "change management," people will automatically adapt. (Example: "We're implementing change management" without understanding that employees may resist change if they don't understand the purpose or fear job insecurity.)

- Used to simply introduce new rules or processes, ignoring the human and cultural aspects of change. (Example: "We are implementing a new change management program" without including employee engagement, feedback loops, and leadership and team alignment.)

Actionable Ways to Make It Meaningful:

✓ **Communicate the "why" behind the change—** Employees are more likely to follow leaders if they understand the purpose and benefits of the change. (Example: Before launching new software, leaders explain how it improves workflows rather than just announcing it.)

✓ **Engage employees early—**Involve teams in decision-making rather than forcing change upon them. (Example: Inviting frontline employees to weigh in on potential workflow changes often leads to smoother adoption and better solutions.)

✓ **Provide training and support—**Offer hands-on workshops to ensure employees feel confident in using new systems. Confidence drives adoption. (Example: Pairing system rollouts with small-group coaching sessions can ease the learning curve and boost long-term usage.)

Growth Mindset

What It Means:

- Believing that abilities, intelligence, and skills can develop over time through effort, learning, and resilience.
- Encouraging continuous improvement, adaptability, and openness to new challenges in individuals and teams.

How It's Often Misused:

- This phrase is used as a slogan but lacks real support for continuous learning and development. (Example: When leaders say "We have a growth mindset culture," but employees fear failure, lack access to training, or receive little constructive feedback, leaving the message empty.)

- Organizations may use this as a catchphrase to push employees to work harder without providing resources or support. (Example: When leaders say "Just have a growth mindset" without providing guidance, coaching, or development opportunities, this phrase becomes an excuse for lack of leadership support rather than a motivator for innovation.)

Actionable Ways to Make It Meaningful:

✓ **Reward learning and effort, not just results**—Growth comes with growing pains; employees must be encouraged to continue having a growth mindset in the face of failure. (Example: Recognizing employees who take on new challenges, even if they don't succeed immediately.)

✓ **Encourage feedback and development**—Leaders should provide constructive coaching instead of just evaluating performance. Growth comes from guidance, not just grading.

✓ **Promote risk-taking in innovation**—Companies can create safe spaces for employees to test new ideas without fear of failure. Progress often starts with permission to experiment.

Breakthrough

What It Means:

- Making a significant and transformative discovery, innovation, or achievement that leads to major progress.
- Finding a solution that overcomes a long-standing barrier—signaling a moment when a difficult problem is solved in a way that wasn't previously possible.

How It's Often Misused:

- Overused to describe minor improvements. (Example: A smartphone company calling a slightly longer battery life a "breakthrough in mobile technology" when it's just a 5 percent increase.)

- Used as a vague, hype-driven promise without clear evidence, making the term feel like empty corporate jargon. (Example: A CEO claiming "We are on the verge of a breakthrough in AI" without concrete details or a timeline.)

Actionable Ways to Make It Meaningful:

✓ **Reserve "breakthrough" for truly transformative advancements—**Labeling every change as a breakthrough can diminish the meaning. (Example: Instead of saying "Our new app update is a breakthrough," reframe by stating that "the update reduces customer onboarding time by 75 percent, solving a long-standing problem.")

✓ **Back it up with data or real-world impact—**Demonstrate how and why the breakthrough is so significant using concrete examples. (Example: "Our research team has achieved a breakthrough: a 65 percent reduction in tumor growth in early clinical trials.")

✓ **Communicate the "before" and "after" differences—**Breakthroughs signal transformation, which should be clearly explained. (Example: "Previously, solar panels could only store energy for eight hours. Our new technology extends that to forty-eight hours, a real breakthrough in making renewable energy viable overnight.")

Scalability

What It Means:

- The ability to grow efficiently without compromising performance or quality.
- A measure of adaptability and cost-effectiveness in expansion.

How It's Often Misused:

- Used to describe any kind of growth, even if inefficient. (Example: "Our hiring process is scalable" when in reality it requires doubling the number of HR staff for every twenty new employees onboarded.)

- Applied vaguely without a clear scalability plan. (Example: "Our platform is fully scalable" but failing to explain to investors how they will handle increased server loads, customer support, or logistics to scale.)

Actionable Ways to Make It Meaningful:

✓ **Define what aspect is scalable and why**—Show the exact changes that will take place and explain why they will make a difference. (Example: Instead of saying "Our digital model is scalable," explain that "the course platform can handle an unlimited number of students without increasing instructor costs, making it highly scalable.")

✓ **Use metrics to demonstrate scalability**—Show that scalability is possible through concrete examples and data. (Example: "Our e-commerce platform processes ten thousand transactions per second with zero downtime, and we can scale to fifty thousand with minimal infrastructure upgrades.")

✓ **Show a real-world example of successful scaling**—Prove that scalability can occur by highlighting past scalable performances. (Example: "Last year, our system supported five thousand users. With the same infrastructure, we now support fifty thousand users with no drop in speed, demonstrating our scalability in action.")

Innovation and Change Comprehensive Case Study: "Too Much Sky, Not Enough Runway"

Scenario

Novalink, a fast-growing digital solutions company, took pride in its creativity. As part of its strategic planning process, the CEO introduced an initiative called NovaNext to shape the company's long-term innovation road map. Leaders were encouraged to bring "blue sky thinking" to the table—ideas unconstrained by current capabilities, timelines, or budgets.

The first few sessions were exhilarating. Teams pitched everything from voice-activated project dashboards to international expansion through a metaverse platform. The leadership team applauded the ambition.

However, once the brainstorming session ended, problems arose. The company lacked a framework for evaluating or implementing ideas. There was no straightforward process for scaling the concepts, no budget to test prototypes, and no road map for turning the vision into reality.

What Went Wrong?

Novalink's culture of innovation had inadvertently created a disconnect between vision and execution.

- **Endless ideation, no filtering**—Dozens of ideas were captured, but none were prioritized. Employees became frustrated as their proposals sat idle or were later deemed "not realistic."

- **Misused resources**—Time and budget were allocated to early-stage experiments without evaluating their scalability. One promising pilot app gained traction but was unable to support enterprise-level use when rolled out.

- **Innovation fatigue**—Teams felt whiplash between expansive thinking and unclear expectations. Without criteria to assess or scale, innovation started to feel like wasted energy rather than meaningful progress.

How Was It Fixed?

To course-correct, Novalink introduced an innovation framework that grounded creativity in feasibility.

- ✓ **Redefined "blue sky thinking"**—Leaders clarified that big ideas were welcome but had to include a path to potential viability. Teams were coached to frame ideas with both aspiration and application in mind.

- ✓ **Introduced a scalability filter**—Before advancing to the funding stage, ideas were assessed for operational impact, tech compatibility, and long-term viability. This ensured that energy was focused on scalable innovation.

- ✓ **Balanced vision with structure**—Novalink created dedicated innovation sprints followed by "reality review" sessions where cross-functional teams evaluated how concepts could move from vision to execution.

Lesson Learned

Creative thinking needs boundaries to produce value. Blue sky thinking can inspire—but without structure, it tends to float away. And not every good idea is scalable. Setting clear criteria and scalable pathways allows companies to innovate effectively and achieve more significant results.

Innovation and Change Snapshot Cases

"Thinking Outside the Box—with No Map Back"

At a creative agency known for its edgy campaigns, the leadership team challenged the staff to "think outside the box" for a significant rebranding pitch to a national retail client. The brief was intentionally vague. Executives told designers, writers, and strategists to "break patterns," "forget about the rules," and "reinvent the idea of campaign." No creative limits. No brand templates. No filters.

The brainstorming sessions were electric. Concepts ranged from augmented reality shopping experiences to a fictional universe built around the client's products. Teams were energized and excited that they had gone big.

But when the final pitch was delivered, the client was bewildered. The presentation lacked cohesion. Though imaginative, the ideas had little connection to the company's identity or customer base. One executive asked flatly, "Did anyone read our brand guidelines?"

Internally, some of the creatives were frustrated too. Their more grounded but still creative ideas had been shelved in favor of flashier, riskier ones. And without structure, the bold thinking had no strategic tether. It was innovation without direction.

Creative freedom needs purpose. "Thinking outside the box" only works when you understand what is inside the box and why it matters. Innovation should solve the right problem, not just look different. Bold isn't always better. Ideas should be both surprising and purposeful. Innovation should elevate relevance, not obscure it.

"Scaling Before the Foundation Set"

A fast-growing telehealth start-up made headlines after securing a significant funding round and announcing plans to "revolutionize virtual care delivery at scale." Leadership leaned heavily on terms like "agile expansion," "frictionless growth," and "digital-first disruption" in their strategic communications. Within months, the company expanded to multiple new states, onboarded dozens of providers, and tripled its user base. The goal? Prove to investors that the business model could scale rapidly and deliver returns.

On paper, the plan looked impressive. But operational cracks quickly emerged: Appointment scheduling systems lagged, support teams were overwhelmed, and compliance documentation was inconsistent across regions. The infrastructure had not kept pace with ambition. The organization had scaled its image faster than its systems. What was intended to be a growth milestone quickly became a recovery mission. Operations scrambled to patch gaps because the company had scaled in numbers but not in readiness.

Growth messaging without operational readiness can create a trust gap between what is promised and what is delivered. Scalability isn't just about size; it's also about stability. Growth that outpaces your foundation puts everything at risk. Build before you boost. Scalability works best when systems can flex, adapt, and support what's coming next, not just what's already in place.

Innovation and Change Buzzwords Summary

Innovation and change buzzwords can drive progress but only when accompanied by clarity, intent, and follow-through. Reference the following list when you need a reminder.

- **Think Outside the Box**—Innovation starts with challenging assumptions.
- **Blue Sky Thinking**—Vision is nothing without execution.
- **Change Management**—Alignment drives successful change.

- **Growth Mindset**—Challenges fuel progress.
- **Breakthrough**—Only truly innovative solutions lead to major progress.
- **Scalability**—Growth must be efficient and effective.

5

COMMUNICATION AND DECISION-MAKING BUZZWORDS

THESE BUZZWORDS ARE USED in meetings and corporate emails.

Clear communication is essential for business success. Yet many corporate conversations are filled with jargon like "touch base" and "deep dive." These phrases are meant to keep conversations efficient but can lead to ambiguity and unnecessary meetings. For example, saying "Let's touch base next week" doesn't specify when or how. Telling someone to "drill down" on a topic without guidance can be unhelpful. Instead of relying on vague terms, effective communicators provide clear instructions and expectations.

Buzzwords and cases in this chapter include the following:

- Transparency
- Data-Driven Decisions
- Deep Dive
- Bandwidth
- Drill Down
- Stakeholder Buy-In
- "The Data Was Right—but the People Weren't Ready" (Comprehensive Case)
- "Transparency Without the Why" (Snapshot Case)
- "The Deep Dive That Derailed the Meeting" (Snapshot Case)

Transparency

What It Means:

- Open and honest communication where employees, stakeholders, or customers can access key information.
- Clear decision-making processes that build trust by eliminating secrecy and uncertainty.

How It's Often Misused:

- Claims transparency without action. Leaders say they're transparent but withhold critical information. (Example: Announcing significant changes but not explaining their reasoning.)

- Confuses transparency with overdisclosure. Sharing excessive or irrelevant details that create confusion rather than clarity. (Example: Leadership sharing personal conflicts instead of focusing on company strategy.)
- Uses transparency as a justification for tough decisions. Instead of genuine openness, transparency is used as an excuse for unpopular choices. (Example: "We're being transparent and cutting 20 percent of staff without further explanation.")

Actionable Ways to Make It Meaningful:

✓ **Communicate decisions with clarity and context—** Transparency builds trust when it is genuine, clear, and purposeful. (Example: Explaining why a policy change is necessary and how it affects employees positively.)

✓ **Balance openness with discretion—**Oversharing is not the same as transparency. (Example: Sharing financial performance updates but protecting sensitive competitive data.)

✓ **Encourage two-way transparency—**Transparency should be reciprocated, showing honesty to others and allowing them to be honest in return. (Example: Creating an open-door policy where employees feel safe voicing concerns.)

Data-Driven Decisions

What It Means:

- Basing business strategies and actions on facts, research, and measurable insights rather than intuition and assumptions.
- Using data analysis to support problem-solving and forecasting for more accurate and effective decision-making.

How It's Often Misused:

- Uses data selectively to confirm biases. Leaders cherry-pick statistics to support a predetermined decision. (Example: Only showing positive survey results while ignoring negative feedback.)

- Relies on data without considering context. Leaders make rigid decisions based on numbers alone. (Example: Laying off employees due to budget cuts without assessing long-term effects on company morale and performance.)
- Confuses quantity with quality. Reports are overloaded with irrelevant data rather than focused on meaningful insights. (Example: Presenting a fifty-slide analytics deck without actionable takeaways.)

Actionable Ways to Make It Meaningful:

✓ **Use data as a guide, not a replacement for judgment—** Data is robust when used to inform thoughtful decisions. (Example: Combining market research with customer feedback to refine product features.)

✓ **Ensure data is accurate and relevant—**Data-driven decisions mean nothing if the data is not true or complete. (Example: Verifying trends over time rather than making decisions based on one data point.)

✓ **Translate data into clear action steps—**The data itself won't tell you what to do. Ensure your information translates to actions. (Example: Instead of reporting website traffic, analyze which content types drive the most engagement and adjust your strategy accordingly.)

Deep Dive

What It Means:

- An in-depth exploration of a topic, process, or issue to uncover detailed insights and solutions.
- A structured analysis that goes beyond surface-level information to identify and address root causes.

How It's Often Misused:

- Used as a stalling tactic. Teams say they'll do a deep dive but never implement findings. (Example: Saying "We need to deep dive into this issue" but you never reconvene with conclusions.)

- Becomes an endless investigation. Spending too much time analyzing without moving to action. (Example: Conducting months of competitor research without launching a new or improved product.)
- Confusing deep dives with unnecessary complexity. Overanalyzing details that don't contribute to meaningful outcomes. (Example: Conducting extensive reports on minor expenses instead of focusing on high-impact decisions.)

Actionable Ways to Make It Meaningful:

- ✓ **Set a clear scope and objective**—Don't fall down the rabbit hole with your research. Look deep but point-edly. (Example: Deep diving into customer retention issues with a defined goal to improve churn rates by 10 percent.)
- ✓ **Balance depth with efficiency**—Too much information can cloud right judgment. Focus on what's most important to the issue at hand. (Example: Analyzing key financial data but focusing only on factors that affect revenue growth.)
- ✓ **Ensure that findings lead to action**—A deep dive should move projects forward, not mire them in endless analysis. (Example: After a deep dive into low employee engagement, implement a structured improvement plan rather than just reporting issues.)

Bandwidth

What It Means:

- An individual's or team's capacity to handle tasks and responsibilities effectively without being overwhelmed.
- A realistic assessment of available resources, time, and energy before committing to new projects.

How It's Often Misused:

- Used as an excuse to avoid responsibility. Saying "We don't have the bandwidth" when prioritization is lacking. (Example: A department claims no bandwidth for innovation while wasting time on unnecessary meetings.)

- Confusing temporary overload with permanent limits. Assuming a busy season means no future flexibility. (Example: Avoiding growth opportunities by assuming every quarter will be as hectic as the busiest one.)
- Lack of strategic planning around bandwidth. Committing to projects without assessing workload realities. (Example: Taking on multiple initiatives without considering available resources.)

Actionable Ways to Make It Meaningful:

✓ **Assess and allocate workloads fairly**—Each person and team has a limit to their bandwidth; ensure you know where that limit is. (Example: If a team is overloaded, reassign tasks instead of overworking individuals.)

✓ **Communicate bandwidth realistically**—Don't assume the team will perform better than they ever have for a new project. Base decisions on past performance. (Example: A manager discusses resource limitations early rather than allowing a project to fail due to lack of capacity.)

✓ **Improve efficiency to free up bandwidth**—Bandwidth can be expanded when simple tasks can be automated. (Example: Automating routine reports to reduce manual work and free up time for strategic initiatives.)

Drill Down

What It Means:

- Breaking down complex information into detailed components to find key insights.
- Focusing on specific data points, patterns, or underlying causes rather than broad overviews.

How It's Often Misused:

- Loses sight of the bigger picture. Drilling down so much that strategic goals are deferred. (Example: Overfocusing on one product's performance while ignoring company-wide profitability.)

- Confuses detail with productivity. Spending too much time on small elements that don't drive results. (Example: A sales team analyzing minor client interactions instead of looking at overall conversion trends.)
- Drills down without action. Investigating problems without implementing solutions. (Example: Constantly reviewing employee engagement data but not making cultural improvements.)

Actionable Ways to Make It Meaningful:

✓ **Define when drilling down is necessary—**Some business decisions will need a deeper look than others. (Example: Analyzing cost breakdowns to identify where a budget is wasted.)

✓ **Use it to uncover real solutions—**Pick a problem area first and then dive deep to uncover solutions for that issue. (Example: Investigating customer complaints to find service gaps and improve satisfaction.)

✓ **Balance detail with decision-making—**Drill down when needed, but don't get lost in the details where it can be difficult to see what decisions to make. (Example: A marketing team analyzing ad performance while reviewing overall ROI to ensure alignment with business goals.)

Stakeholder Buy-In

What It Means:

- Gaining support and approval from key decision-makers, teams, or customers before moving forward with a plan.
- Building trust and alignment so that initiatives succeed with full backing and support.

How It's Often Misused:

- Assumes buy-in is automatic, often announcing changes without real engagement. (Example: A company rolls out a new policy without consulting affected teams.)

- Confuses buy-in with compliance. People may agree publicly but resist privately. (Example: Employees say they support a new initiative but quietly disengage.)
- Forces agreement instead of earning it. Pushes a decision without addressing concerns. (Example: Leadership demands buy-in without explaining the value of the strategy.)

Actionable Ways to Make It Meaningful:

✓ **Engage stakeholders early**—Buy-in should be earned through engagement, not just expected. (Example: Involve teams in strategy discussions rather than just informing them afterward.)

✓ **Address issues and concerns openly**—Forcing buy-in leads to future issues, but addressing questions head-on guarantees everyone is on the same page. (Example: Holding Q&A sessions to ensure buy-in is based on real understanding.)

✓ **Show and explain the value of the decision**—People will follow along enthusiastically when you explain how the decision affects their day-to-day in a valuable way. (Example: Demonstrating how a new software implementation will improve efficiency and reduce workload.)

Communication and Decision-Making Comprehensive Case Study: "The Data Was Right—but the People Weren't Ready"

Scenario

At EnvisionEd, an education technology firm, the product team conducted a thorough analytics review of its flagship learning platform. Usage data revealed a clear pattern: Students were engaging more with interactive content modules and spending less time on static, PDF-based lessons. The data was compelling—conversion rates were higher, satisfaction scores increased, and learning outcomes improved where interactive content was used.

The team made a confident recommendation to pivot the product strategy based on data-driven decisions, phasing out static modules in favor of interactive formats. The plan was sound, grounded in evidence, and aligned with long-term goals. But when it was rolled out to partner schools and internal sales teams, the reaction was mixed. Adoption lagged. Teachers raised concerns, and regional sales reps quietly resisted the change.

Leadership was surprised. They had made the "right" call, so why wasn't it sticking?

What Went Wrong?

Despite the strength of the data, stakeholder buy-in had been neglected.

- **Lack of contextual output**—While the data team had robust metrics, they had not gathered on-the-ground insights from teachers or school administrators. These stakeholders felt their practical concerns had been ignored, especially around training and access to devices.

- **Change without conversation**—The announcement came as a directive, not a dialogue. Schools and internal teams were informed but not involved. Some felt blindsided.

- **Misalignment on readiness**—Sales teams weren't equipped to explain the shift in strategy. Teachers hadn't received demos or training on the interactive content. As a result, there was pushback—even from those who supported the idea in principle. The data may have been precise, but the path to adoption wasn't.

How Was It Fixed?

Realizing the disconnect, EnvisionEd paused the rollout and restructured its approach.

- ✓ **Reframed data as a starting point**—Leaders clarified that data wasn't a conclusion—it was an invitation to understand the underlying reasons. Product teams hosted listening sessions with educators and partners to gather qualitative input that enriched the numbers.

✓ **Engaged stakeholders early**—New pilot programs were launched with a small group of schools, who were given a seat at the table. Their feedback shaped refinements to the content and implementation process.

✓ **Created shared ownership**—Internal training was launched alongside new messaging that emphasized the "why" behind the shift. Sales and support teams became advocates rather than messengers. Buy-in increased, and adoption followed.

Lesson Learned

Good data doesn't guarantee good decisions, especially if people aren't ready to act on them. Evidence must be paired with empathy. Stakeholder buy-in isn't a checkbox—it's the foundation of change. To lead with data, you still need to lead with people.

Communication and Decision-Making Snapshot Cases

"Transparency Without the Why"

A leading consumer electronics firm, amid a sudden restructuring, sent an all-staff email announcing the elimination of several product lines and a reduction in the workforce. The message emphasized the company's commitment to "transparency," noting that they were "sharing this information early to be open with employees."

While the message was factually open, it lacked context. Employees were left wondering why the decisions were made, the strategic rationale, and how it aligned with the company's long-term goals. Morale dropped sharply, and internal chatter filled the vacuum of unanswered questions. Transparency without clarity led to confusion and distrust.

The leadership believed they were modeling openness by communicating the changes quickly. But "transparency" without the why often reads as cold disclosure. Employees didn't just want information—they wanted insight, reassurance, and shared direction. By omitting the human and strategic narrative, the company unintentionally heightened anxiety.

Transparency is more than releasing information; it is about explaining decisions in a way that builds trust and connection.

"The Deep Dive That Derailed the Meeting"

At a strategic planning offsite, a senior analyst was asked to "take a deep dive" into market expansion options. She prepared a detailed forty-slide presentation filled with charts, frameworks, and competitive data. Her session, scheduled for thirty minutes, ran over an hour and derailed the rest of the day's agenda.

The "deep dive" lacked framing. Without a clear purpose or decision point, the group became overwhelmed with information instead of empowered to act. Key priorities and discussions were postponed, and energy in the room plummeted.

The phrase "deep dive" sounds impressive, but in practice, it requires structure. The analyst did her job, thorough research, but the request itself was too open-ended. Deep dives should uncover clarity, not bury it. When leadership uses this phrase, they must define the goal. Are we evaluating? Comparing? Validating a direction?

A successful deep dive is not about how much you present, but how well it leads to insight and action.

Communication and Decision-Making Buzzwords Summary

These buzzwords, used in meetings and corporate emails, are meant to keep conversations efficient but can sometimes come across as empty jargon. Reference the following list when you need a reminder.

- **Transparency**—Trust comes from clear, honest communication.
- **Data-Driven Decisions**—Use data wisely, with context and strategy.
- **Deep Dive**—Dig deep but turn insights into action.

- **Bandwidth**—Plan your workload and don't hide behind excuses.
- **Drill Down**—Focus on details but keep the big picture in mind.
- **Stakeholder Buy-In**—Earn buy-in through engagement.

6

HONORABLE MENTIONS: BUZZWORDS WORTH NOTING

THIS CHAPTER FEATURES BUZZWORDS that didn't receive complete analysis in earlier sections but still play a noticeable role in today's workplace language. These are terms you'll hear in meetings, see in strategy documents, and encounter in casual office conversations—phrases that are familiar, functional, and sometimes a little hazy. Rather than deconstructing them in depth, this section provides brief, narrative-style reflections on each term, highlighting their everyday use, potential pitfalls, and strategies for making them more purposeful in professional settings.

While many of these buzzwords serve legitimate functions when used intentionally, they also tend to drift into habit or filler. This section encourages readers to pause, reflect, and decide which terms enhance their message and which ones could be reconsidered or replaced. These short commentaries are designed to be quick reads with practical takeaways.

To add clarity and structure, we've grouped them into four practical clusters based on how they tend to function in business settings. Whether used to connect with others, define strategy, signal value, or shape workplace culture, each phrase carries potential but only when backed by real intent and clarity.

To close out the chapter, we've also included a few buzzwords that add a touch of levity to the mix. These aren't about business efficiency or leadership lingo—they're the colorful metaphors and quirky phrases that tend to show up with a wink. Whether it's "herding cats" or "pushing the envelope," these expressions add humor, personality, and occasional absurdity to workplace communication. They serve as reminders that language isn't just about clarity; it's also about culture, tone, and knowing your audience.

Cluster 1: Communication and Collaboration

These phrases show up in quick check-ins, emails, or meetings. They aim to promote openness and alignment, but without clarity, they can feel routine or hollow. Use them to encourage genuine connection and shared understanding.

Touch Base

A staple in professional conversations, "touch base" is used as a casual way to check in or follow up on a task or discussion. It suggests an informal exchange of updates but can be frustratingly vague. Using it too often without specifying the reason or timing can leave the other party unsure of the next steps. To make it effective, clarify the purpose: "Let's touch base on the budget details this Friday to finalize the next steps." This minor adjustment turns an ambiguous phrase into meaningful communication.

Run It up the Flagpole

This phrase implies casually presenting an idea to gauge its potential usefulness for informal brainstorming or soft feedback. It's also a convenient way to suggest action without taking responsibility. If you're going to "run it up the flagpole," be clear who's seeing it, what kind of feedback you want, and what happens next. Avoid using it as a deflection—clarity and follow-through matter more than clever phrasing.

On the Same Page

Often used to signal alignment, this phrase assumes a shared understanding—but rarely confirms it. Teams may nod along while interpreting the "page" differently. To make this expression meaningful, back it up with documented agreements, clarified priorities, or next steps. Alignment isn't achieved by saying it—it's achieved by doing it.

Open Door Policy

"Open door policy" is a well-intentioned phrase meant to suggest transparency and approachability. But in many organizations, the "open door" is more symbolic than real. Busy leaders, unwelcoming tones, or unclear follow-through can undermine it. For this term to carry weight, leaders must actively demonstrate they are available, responsive, and willing to engage meaningfully when someone walks through that proverbial door.

Cluster 2: Strategy and Planning

Often found in presentations and planning sessions, these terms suggest big-picture thinking or flexibility. But they're only effective when anchored in fundamental analysis and actionable direction, not just aspirational language.

Game Plan

An intense "game plan" provides structure to an initiative, outlining clear steps for execution. But it can become an empty phrase when used loosely—"Let's devise a game plan"—without follow-through. Pair it with specifics to ensure it drives action: "Let's finalize the game plan for the product launch by Friday, including marketing and sales targets for Q1."

Pivot

Popularized by the start-up world, "pivot" describes a strategic shift in direction based on market changes or new insights. While necessary at times, it is often misused when leaders make frequent, reactive changes without clear reasoning. A real "pivot" should be intentional and data-driven, such as: "Given the declining user engagement, we are pivoting toward a subscription-based model after testing positive responses from our pilot program."

Think Tank

Organizations use "think tank" to describe a group dedicated to brainstorming innovative solutions. While the term conveys high-level problem-solving, it loses impact when misapplied to unfocused meetings that lack structure. A successful "think tank" should yield actionable outcomes, not just discussions. For example: "This quarter, our product innovation think tank will identify two new features we can prototype for early customer testing."

Take a Thirty-Thousand-Foot View

This phrase is useful when encouraging big-picture thinking but can also be used dismissively to avoid engaging with details. Leaders should strike a balance between strategic vision and execution. Instead of saying "Let's take a thirty-thousand-foot view," clarify what needs to be examined: "Let's take a step back and assess how our customer experience aligns with our brand promise before making design changes."

Fail Fast

Once a hallmark of Silicon Valley innovation, the concept of "fail fast" encourages rapid experimentation and iteration. In theory, it's about minimizing waste and learning quickly. In practice, however, it can be used to justify poor planning or insufficient due diligence. True innovation doesn't celebrate failure—it celebrates learning. Use this phrase when a framework is in place to reflect, adjust, and apply what has been learned.

Cluster 3: Value and Impact

These expressions emphasize results, progress, and contribution. They work best when tied to what's being delivered, why it matters, and who benefits. Without that, they risk becoming performance theater.

Quick Win

Leaders often encourage teams to focus on "quick wins" to build momentum. While valuable, overemphasizing small victories can sometimes shift attention away from long-term priorities. Instead of calling everything a quick win, use the term for tasks with low effort but high impact, such as "Let's start with a quick win by simplifying our onboarding emails to reduce customer confusion immediately."

Value-Add

"Value-add" is commonly used to highlight an additional benefit that enhances a product, service, or process. However, it becomes a filler phrase when overused without specifying the actual value. Instead of stating "This feature is a great value-add," clarify why by saying "This new reporting tool adds value by reducing manual tracking time by 40 percent."

Value Proposition

A staple in strategy and marketing conversations, "value proposition" is meant to clarify what makes a product or service distinct and worthwhile. Yet it's often used as a placeholder—more buzz than clarity. If someone says "What's our value proposition?" and no one can answer plainly, the issue isn't the term; it's the lack of meaning behind it.

Action Item

"Let's identify action items" is common in meetings, but follow-through matters. Too often, action items appear in recap emails without names, deadlines, or clarity. The term isn't the problem; the ambiguity is. When well-defined, it drives accountability. When vague, it just clutters the list.

Deliverables

"Deliverables" signals concrete progress—something to be completed, reviewed, or submitted. But like many project terms, it can get lost in abstraction. "We need to hit our deliverables" only works when everyone knows what they are, by when, and in what form. Otherwise, it's just a vague reminder to stay busy.

Cluster 4: Culture and Mindset

These buzzwords reflect the kind of workplace people want to be part of—innovative, efficient, and aligned. But culture isn't created by slogans. These phrases only resonate when supported by clear expectations and shared behaviors.

Elevator Pitch

A well-crafted "elevator pitch" is crucial in networking and sales, as it provides a concise and compelling explanation of an idea, product, or service—theoretically fast enough to say before the elevator arrives at your floor. However, when over-rehearsed or too generic, it loses its effectiveness. A great pitch should be tailored to the audience, remaining natural and focused: "We help businesses streamline logistics by reducing supply chain inefficiencies. Let me share a quick example of how we achieve that."

Customer-Centric

Often heard in mission statements, "customer-centric" sounds great—and is easy to say. But without meaningful systems or frontline behavior to support it, the term rings hollow. It earns its place when it guides decisions and actions. Until then, it's more aspiration than reality. Instead, leaders should say "Let's take a step back and assess how our customer experience aligns with our brand promise before making design changes."

Disruptive Thinking

"Disruptive thinking" is a popular concept in innovation discussions, suggesting a bold and transformative approach to industry norms. However, it often gets diluted when minor improvements are labeled as "disruptive." To avoid this, reserve the term for breakthrough ideas: "This AI-driven platform is disrupting the traditional hiring process by reducing recruitment time by 70 percent."

Work Smarter, Not Harder

This motivational phrase is often tossed into conversations as if it alone will unlock efficiency. While it promotes the right mindset—prioritizing strategic effort over sheer volume—it often lacks follow-through. Teams hear it but are rarely provided with the tools to work smarter. When used, leaders should pair it with actual systems or workflows that support more brilliant (not just harder) ways to achieve goals. It often lacks real-world strategies to support it. Teams benefit more from hearing how to do that, not just the mantra.

Culture Fit

This buzzword is often used in hiring and team building to suggest that a person's values or personality align with those of the organization. At its best, it reflects an intentional effort to build cohesive, collaborative teams. However, the term can also become a catch-all, used vaguely or even defensively to justify rejecting candidates who think differently. Without a careful definition, "culture fit" can reinforce sameness and undermine efforts to build diverse and dynamic teams. To use it meaningfully, companies must clearly define their culture based on a shared purpose, values, and behaviors, rather than personal similarities or comfort levels.

Buzzwords with a Wink

Even the most seasoned professionals need to chuckle at the language we use. These buzzwords walk the line between metaphor and exaggeration—and yet, they persist in meetings, emails, and watercooler conversations. Here are five that always seem to find their way into the mix, often with a raised eyebrow or a grin.

Circle the Wagons

A frontier-inspired way to say "Let's regroup and protect ourselves from outside threats." Sounds heroic, but it's usually used to rally a team around a bad Q4 result or a tricky client. Dramatic? Absolutely. Useful? Occasionally.

Push the Envelope

Borrowed from aviation, this phrase is meant to inspire bold thinking. But in corporate halls, it's usually code for "Let's try something slightly riskier than usual—unless someone objects." A classic, if slightly overplayed.

Herding Cats

Used to describe managing chaotic projects or teams with strong personalities. It's an oddly accurate, endearingly visual phrase and a go-to for anyone managing a cross-functional initiative with no apparent owner. Bonus points if there are actual cats on the team Slack channel.

Thought Shower

An alternative to "brainstorm" that attempts to sound modern, inclusive, or just different. It rarely lands and sometimes raises more questions than it provides answers. Still, it's earned a spot for sheer audacity.

Drink the Kool-Aid

A phrase that implies deep (sometimes imprudent) loyalty to a leader or company vision. It's often said half-jokingly by people who have attended one too many all-hands meetings. Use with caution—it's edgy, and not everyone finds it amusing. Its origins trace back to the tragic 1978 Jonestown cult deaths—a sobering reminder of why this expression deserves careful handling.

Final Thought

We've all said these and heard them too many times. They're part of the corporate lexicon, for better or worse. The key isn't to avoid them entirely, but to be aware of how they land, what they imply, and when a more explicit message might make the job even better.

7

BRINGING IT ALL TOGETHER

LANGUAGE IS MORE THAN A TOOL—it's a reflection of how we think, how we lead, and how we connect. Throughout this book, we've looked closer at the corporate buzzwords that fill meeting rooms, slide decks, strategy sessions, and casual conversations. Some of these phrases carry accurate weight when used well. Others have drifted into habit—familiar but vague and repeated without reflection.

This guide wasn't written to eliminate buzzwords. It was written to reclaim their power, to help professionals use language more intentionally, clearly, and confidently. When communication is specific, honest, and grounded in purpose, it drives action, creates alignment, and builds trust.

We've covered thirty-one widely used buzzwords in depth, explored nineteen more through narrative insight, and ended with a handful of humorous expressions that remind us not to take ourselves too seriously. The message has remained consistent along the way: Words matter because clarity is leadership.

Throughout this journey, we also explored real-world cases where corporate buzzwords played a pivotal role, sometimes creating alignment and occasionally confusing it. These stories offered more than anecdotes; they revealed patterns of behavior and miscommunication that affect teams, projects, and trust. The broad lesson? Language shapes action. When words are used carelessly, even with good intentions, they can mislead. When they're chosen wisely, they clarify, connect, and drive meaningful results.

What This Book Delivers

This book is more than a glossary of jargon or a critique of trendy language. It's a practical guide designed to help professionals strengthen communication, enhance leadership credibility, and improve clarity across all interaction channels.

You've explored in-depth buzzword assessments, narrative insights, real-world cases, and tools that invite reflection and action. Remember, the intent isn't to eliminate buzzwords; it's to help you use them intentionally and powerfully. Here's what this book provides:

- A fresh lens on how everyday phrases influence leadership, culture, and decision-making

- A framework for turning vague or overused terms into meaningful, action-driven language
- Real-world case studies that show how buzzwords affect outcomes—positively or negatively
- Self-awareness tools to evaluate your habits and word choices
- A practical toolkit for building better conversations, meetings, and messages
- A balance of depth and levity, so communication feels authentic
- A challenge and an invitation to become the kind of communicator others trust, follow, and remember

This guide equips you with definitions, discipline, strategy, and confidence in how you use language every day.

Put Your Words to Work

Now it's your turn. Let this guide be the beginning, not the end, of how you approach language with purpose.

✓ Review your buzzword habits. Use the self-audit as a seasonal check-in.
✓ Facilitate better communication within your team. Try the toolkit exercises in your next meeting.
✓ Replace one vague phrase a week. Make it clear, specific, and purposeful.

✓ Model intentional language. Your example sets the tone more than your title.

✓ Use the reflection tools to coach others. Help teammates rethink their language habits.

✓ Keep learning and improving. Language and business trends shift over time. Stay adaptable and continue to refine how you communicate.

Clear communication isn't about perfection. It's about presence, purpose, and connection. The better we say what we mean, the better we lead, listen, and build.

Thank you for reading this book. Now put your words to work, wisely.

Final Takeaways

- **Buzzwords can be helpful or hollow**—Their power lies in how, when, and why we use them.
- **Clarity builds trust**—Confusing jargon, however clever, undermines connection.
- **Language shapes culture**—The words you choose influence the tone of your team, your meetings, and your brand.
- **Humor has its place**—Recognizing the absurdity of some phrases doesn't weaken your credibility; it strengthens your authenticity.

- **Reflection changes behavior**—The exercises, self-audits, and toolkit can help you turn insight into habit.

- **Communication is a leadership skill**—And like all skills, it requires regular, thoughtful practice.

Strategic Buzzword Toolkit: Beyond the Pages

CONTENTS

Strategic Buzzword Toolkit

INTRODUCTION TO THE TOOLKIT

A Practical Resource for Clearer, More Intentional Communication

IN TODAY'S FAST-MOVING BUSINESS ENVIRONMENT, the words we choose have the power to clarify—or to confuse.

Buzzwords can either strengthen understanding or dilute meaning, depending on how thoughtfully they are used.

The Strategic Buzzword Toolkit is designed to move you beyond theory. It provides practical exercises, assessments, and reflection tools to help you build stronger communication habits. Whether leading a team, preparing a presentation, or simply aiming to communicate more purposefully, this Toolkit is your companion in becoming a more transparent, credible, and strategic communicator.

Purpose

The purpose of the Strategic Buzzword Toolkit is simple: This is to help you use language more intentionally so that your words connect, clarify, and lead. Through a series of self-assessments, reflection questions, and exercises, you will sharpen your awareness, refine your skills, and strengthen your ability to communicate with focus and authenticity. You will notice that the buzzwords featured in the Toolkit do not exactly match the buzzwords discussed earlier in the book. This is intentional. In the real world, buzzwords appear in various forms—some common, some emerging, and others tailored to specific industries or settings. The activities provided here are designed to reflect that broader landscape and help you practice understanding the type of language you will likely encounter in business and professional environments.

What's Included in the Toolkit

- Assessments to evaluate your current buzzword habits and clarity of communication
- Reflection prompts to deepen your understanding of how language shapes leadership and credibility
- Exercises and skill builders to practice clearer, more effective communication strategies
- Bonus tools to extend your learning and apply strategic thinking to buzzword use

How to Use This Toolkit

There is no single "right" way to move through the Toolkit.

You may want to complete the assessments first to establish a baseline, then spend time reflecting, and finally work through the exercises to build practical skills. Alternatively, you might choose one or two sections that align most closely with your immediate goals.

Use the Toolkit as a guide, a challenge, and a resource. Return to it whenever you want to refresh your communication approach or recalibrate your leadership voice.

Summary

Clear language reflects clear thinking. This Toolkit is an invitation to think more deeply about your words—and to use them as powerful tools for clarity, trust, and leadership.

Strategic Buzzword Toolkit

ASSESSMENT SECTION

Assessing Your Buzzword Awareness, Clarity, and Appropriateness

THIS SECTION FEATURES three carefully designed assessments to help you reflect on your use of buzzwords—how often you use them, how clearly you express them, and whether they fit the context. Use these assessments to sharpen your communication skills and identify areas for improvement.

Buzzword Usage Self-Rating Scale

Purpose:

To help users reflect on how often they rely on common business buzzwords in daily spoken and written communication.

Instructions:

Review the following list of buzzwords. For each one, rate how frequently you use it in your everyday professional communication based on the following scale:

1. Rarely
2. Occasionally
3. Sometimes
4. Often
5. Constantly

Be honest about your natural speaking and writing habits. This exercise is not about judgment but about increasing awareness.

- Synergy: _____
- Low-Hanging Fruit: _____
- Scalability: _____
- Win-Win: _____
- Bandwidth: _____
- Drill Down: _____
- Leverage: _____
- Strategic Alignment: _____
- Value Proposition: _____
- Deep Dive: _____
- Disruptive: _____
- Innovative: _____

- Circle Back: _____
- Buy-In: _____
- Empower: _____
- Think Outside the Box: _____
- Touch Base: _____
- Transparency: _____
- Game Changer: _____
- Move the Needle: _____

Reflection Prompts:

- Which buzzwords do you tend to use most often?
- Are you choosing them out of habit or because they strengthen your communication?
- Are there clearer or more precise alternatives you could use?

Buzzword Clarity Scale

Purpose:

To help users evaluate how clearly and meaningfully they use common buzzwords in their professional communication.

Instructions:

Review the following list of buzzwords. For each buzzword, rate your typical clarity of use based on the following scale:

1. Vague or Confusing
2. Unclear
3. Adequate
4. Clear
5. Very Clear and Purposeful

Be honest and self-critical—the goal is to identify opportunities to be more precise.

- Synergy: _____
- Low-Hanging Fruit: _____
- Scalability: _____
- Win-Win: _____
- Bandwidth: _____
- Drill Down: _____
- Leverage: _____
- Strategic Alignment: _____
- Value Proposition: _____
- Deep Dive: _____
- Disruptive: _____
- Innovative: _____
- Circle Back: _____
- Buy-In: _____
- Empower: _____
- Think Outside the Box: _____
- Touch Base: _____

- Transparency: _____
- Game Changer: _____
- Move the Needle: _____

Reflection Prompts:

- Which buzzwords did you score yourself lowest on?
- Why might they come across as vague when you use them?
- How can you make your usage of these terms clearer or more specific?

Context Appropriateness Quiz

Purpose:

To test your judgment about whether a buzzword is used appropriately in a specific situation.

Instructions:

Review each of the following scenarios. Decide whether the buzzword used is appropriate, inappropriate, or could be improved. Select your answer and briefly explain your reasoning.

Answer Choices:

- Appropriate
- Inappropriate
- Could Be Improved

1. Our new app is a true game changer that will revolutionize how users log in.

   ☐ Appropriate
   ☐ Inappropriate
   ☐ Could Be Improved

Reason: _____

2. Let's circle back next week to finalize the executive summary.

   ☐ Appropriate
   ☐ Inappropriate
   ☐ Could Be Improved

Reason: _____

3. We need to drill down on our mission statement before launching this campaign.

   ☐ Appropriate
   ☐ Inappropriate
   ☐ Could Be Improved

Reason: _____

4. This project has strong synergy with our ongoing compliance audit.

☐ Appropriate
☐ Inappropriate
☐ Could Be Improved

Reason: _____

5. Let's touch base after you've met with the legal team.

☐ Appropriate
☐ Inappropriate
☐ Could Be Improved

Reason: _____

6. To move the needle, we need to brainstorm radically different solutions.

☐ Appropriate
☐ Inappropriate
☐ Could Be Improved

Reason: _____

7. It's crucial we gain stakeholder buy-in before announcing layoffs.

☐ Appropriate
☐ Inappropriate
☐ Could Be Improved

Reason: _____

8. We need to empower employees to hit Q2 sales targets by offering bonuses.

☐ Appropriate
☐ Inappropriate
☐ Could Be Improved

Reason: _____

9. The platform needs more bandwidth to support these integrations.

☐ Appropriate
☐ Inappropriate
☐ Could Be Improved

Reason: _____

10. That idea isn't scalable unless we
add international suppliers.

☐ Appropriate
☐ Inappropriate
☐ Could Be Improved

Reason: _____

Context Appropriateness Quiz—Answer Key

Below are suggested answers with explanations for each scenario. Use this section to reflect on your choices and reasoning.

1. Best Answer: Could Be Improved
Explanation: While "game changer" can be powerful, it's often overused. Unless the app truly transforms the user experience, a more specific description would be clearer.

2. Best Answer: Appropriate
Explanation: "Circle back" is commonly accepted in professional settings for revisiting a topic. It fits well for scheduling future discussion.

3. Best Answer: Appropriate
Explanation: "Drill down" suggests a deeper analysis, fitting well when reviewing a mission statement.

4. Best Answer: Inappropriate
Explanation: "Synergy" usually describes combined forces producing greater outcomes. Compliance audits are formal checks, so synergy feels awkward here.

5. Best Answer: Appropriate
Explanation: "Touch base" is an informal but accepted phrase for quick follow-up communication.

6. Best Answer: Appropriate

Explanation: "Move the needle" implies making a significant difference. Brainstorming new solutions fits this context well.

7. Best Answer: Appropriate

Explanation: "Buy-in" is appropriate when describing securing support before major decisions like layoffs.

8. Best Answer: Could Be Improved

Explanation: While "empower" sounds positive, it's slightly vague here. Bonuses incentivize behavior more than empower intrinsic motivation.

9. Best Answer: Appropriate

Explanation: In technical settings, "bandwidth" properly refers to system capacity needs.

10. Best Answer: Appropriate

Explanation: "Scalable" correctly describes efficient expansion potential, fitting the supply chain context.

SUMMARY OF ANSWERS:

1. Could Be Improved
2. Appropriate
3. Appropriate
4. Inappropriate

5. Appropriate
6. Appropriate
7. Appropriate
8. Could Be Improved
9. Appropriate
10. Appropriate

Strategic Buzzword Toolkit

REFLECTION CORNER

Sharpening Your Perspective

THE REFLECTION CORNER is designed to help you think deeply about how language shapes your leadership, communication habits, and professional presence. Each prompt invites you to explore your own buzzword use and sharpen your awareness.

Take time with each question. There are no correct answers—only insights that help you become a more thoughtful and strategic communicator.

Five Reflection Prompts

1) Words That Helped—or Hurt

Consider when a buzzword you used helped clarify your message versus when it unintentionally confused your audience. What made the difference?

2) Your Automatic Buzzwords

What buzzwords do you find yourself using automatically, without thinking? Are there certain situations where you tend to overuse them?

3) Clarity Over Cleverness

Have you ever used a buzzword because it sounded impressive rather than because it made your meaning clearer? How could you have communicated more plainly?

4) The Buzzword That Best Reflects You

Which buzzword (if any) authentically represents your leadership style, communication philosophy, or personal brand? Why?

5) Buzzwords Across the Organization

Observe the buzzwords used by teams, leaders, or departments across your organization. Are they adding focus or creating noise? What patterns do you notice?

Final Thought

Clear communication isn't about eliminating buzzwords; it's about using language that connects, clarifies, and drives purpose. Your words reflect your thinking. Your thinking reflects your leadership.

Strategic Buzzword Toolkit

HANDS-ON PRACTICE: STRATEGIC BUZZWORD EXERCISES

THE HANDS-ON PRACTICE SECTION is where buzzword learning becomes actionable. These exercises are designed to challenge, refine, and reinforce how you think about buzzwords in real-world communication. Whether you're rewriting phrases, choosing the right term for the right moment, or spotting empty language, each activity helps strengthen your clarity and intent.

Why Use This Section:

- To move from passive learning to active skill-building
- To sharpen your ability to communicate with purpose

- To practice strategic language choices in realistic contexts
- To gain confidence in replacing jargon with clarity and substance

These exercises are ideal for individual development, group workshops, or leadership training. Take them seriously—but feel free to enjoy the challenge.

Exercise 1: Buzzword vs. Meaning Matching Game

Purpose

This exercise helps sharpen your understanding of core business terms and their real meaning. Strong communicators use buzzwords appropriately and clearly. Match each buzzword to the correct definition by writing the matching letter (A–O) next to each buzzword.

Buzzwords

1. Synergy
2. Scalability
3. Drill Down
4. Buy-In
5. Low-Hanging Fruit
6. Deep Dive
7. Leverage

8. Transparency
9. Disruptive
10. Value Proposition
11. Circle Back
12. Bandwidth
13. Thought Leadership
14. Empower
15. Win-Win

Definitions

a. Setting an example of innovation, expertise, or future thinking
b. Conducting a thorough, in-depth analysis of a topic or situation
c. Being open, honest, and clear in communication
d. Creating a product, service, or idea that radically changes an industry
e. Ability to grow operations or services smoothly as demand increases
f. Gaining agreement, approval, or commitment from others
g. Using existing resources or relationships to maximum advantage
h. Achieving better results by combining efforts or strengths
i. Giving people the tools, authority, or confidence to act independently

j. Revisiting an issue later to complete or finalize details

k. Capacity or available resources (especially time, attention, or ability)

l. Pursuing the easiest, quickest opportunities first

m. A solution that benefits all parties involved equally

n. The unique benefit a product or service offers to customers

o. Examining an issue or problem in more detail

Answer Key

The table below summarizes the correct answers and the meaning for each buzzword.

Buzzword	Correct Letter	Meaning Summary
Synergy	h	Combining efforts for best results
Scalability	e	Growing efficiently as demand increases
Drill Down	o	Looking into details
Buy-In	f	Gaining agreement or commitment
Low-Hanging Fruit	l	Easy, quick wins
Deep Dive	b	Thorough, deep analysis
Leverage	g	Maximizing use of resources
Transparency	c	Clear, open communication
Disruptive	d	Changing an industry radically
Value Proposition	n	Unique customer benefit
Circle Back	j	Return to a topic later
Bandwidth	k	Capacity or available resources
Thought Leadership	a	Setting an example through expertise
Empower	i	Giving authority or confidence
Win-Win	m	Mutually beneficial outcome

Exercise 2: Jargon-Free Communication Checklist

Purpose

To help professionals ensure their communication is clear, direct, and free of unnecessary jargon that might confuse or distract the audience.

Checklist

CLARITY AND SIMPLICITY

- Have I stated my main point clearly and early?
- Have I removed any complicated words that could be said more simply?

AUDIENCE AWARENESS

- Have I considered what my audience already knows— and what they might not?
- Have I explained any specialized terms or avoided them if unnecessary?

FOCUSED LANGUAGE

- Does each sentence carry only one main idea?
- Have I trimmed any excessive or repetitive wording?

BUZZWORD CONTROL

- Have I limited the use of buzzwords to only when they add meaning?
- Have I replaced buzzwords with plain terms when possible?

CONCRETE EXAMPLES

- Have I used clear examples or data points instead of generalizations?
- Will the reader or listener easily understand what I'm referencing?

TONE AND PROFESSIONALISM

- Is my tone professional, respectful, and direct?
- Does my word choice build credibility rather than trying to impress?

VISUAL CLUTTER

- Have I avoided long paragraphs or dense blocks of text?
- Is essential information easy to spot (bullets, bolding, headings)?

FLUFF REDUCTION

- Have I cut out empty phrases like "at the end of the day," "moving forward," or "paradigm shift"?
- Is every sentence necessary for my message?

STRONG CLOSINGS

- Have I ended with a clear action step, decision, or next move?
- Will my final message leave no confusion about expectations?

Takeaways

Strong communicators respect their audience's time and attention. Before sending your message, ask yourself:

- Is this as clear and simple as it could be?
- Does this truly reflect my intended tone and purpose?
- Have I removed anything that might dilute or confuse my message?

Exercise 3: Choosing Clarity— Best Message Selection

Purpose
To sharpen decision-making skills by selecting the clearest, most effective communication from a set of choices.

Instructions
For each of the following situations, you are given two versions of a communication. Choose the version (A or B) that communicates most clearly, directly, and effectively. Briefly explain why you selected your choice. No answer key is provided. This exercise is for self-reflection, with no right or wrong answers.

Situations

1. Project Update

    a. We need to work together to develop new deliverables that will better meet client needs.

    b. We need to leverage our collective synergies to ideate next-gen deliverables for client satisfaction moving forward.

Your Choice: _____ (A or B)

Reason for Choice: _____

2. Meeting Scheduling

    a. Let's touch base later this week to circle back on the operational alignment points.

    b. Let's meet Thursday to review and finalize our operations plan.

Your Choice: _____ (A or B)

Reason for Choice: _____

3. New Initiative Launch

    a. Our objective is to disrupt the competitive landscape by empowering holistic ecosystems across verticals.

    b. Our goal is to offer new services that meet customer needs better than competitors.

Your Choice: _____ (A or B)

Reason for Choice: _____

4. Request for Action

    a. Please prioritize the easiest tasks first to deliver quick, early results.

    b. Please operationalize the low-hanging fruit ASAP to maximize near-term wins.

Your Choice: _____ (A or B)

Reason for Choice: _____

5. Team Motivation

    a. Let's work together across teams to find new ideas and improve key results.

    b. Let's drive stakeholder engagement and foster cross-functional ideation to amplify KPIs.

Your Choice: _____ (A or B)

Reason for Choice: _____

Strategic Buzzword Toolkit

BONUS SKILL BUILDERS

Applying Buzzword Clarity and Strategy in Action

To FURTHER SHARPEN YOUR COMMUNICATION SKILLS, the following Bonus Skill Builders offer additional ways to apply what you've learned.

The Buzzword Awareness Tool invites you to consider simpler, clearer alternatives to common buzzwords, helping you become a more mindful communicator.

The Buzzword Strategy Match challenges you to think strategically about when—and how—to use buzzwords effectively based on real-world business situations.

These short exercises are designed to strengthen your ability to communicate with precision, credibility, and purpose.

Bonus Skill Builder 1: Buzzword Awareness Tool—What You Say Matters

Purpose

To raise awareness of when buzzwords are used automatically—and to encourage clearer, simpler alternatives where appropriate.

Instructions

For each buzzword listed, review the plain English alternative. When communicating, ask yourself: Would my audience understand this better if I used the plain version?

Buzzword Awareness Tool (15 Examples)

Buzzword	Plain Language Alternative
Leverage	Use, take advantage of
Low-Hanging Fruit	Easy opportunity, quick win
Bandwidth	Time, capacity
Synergy	Working together effectively
Circle Back	Follow up later
Thought Leadership	Expertise, recognized authority
Disruptive	Innovative
Deep Dive	Thorough analysis

Buzzword	Plain Language Alternative
Touch Base	Meet briefly, reconnect
Scalability	Ability to grow or expand easily
Buy-In	Agreement, support
Drill Down	Explore details carefully
Empower	Give authority, build confidence
Win-Win	Mutually beneficial
Value Proposition	Unique advantage, customer benefit

Bonus Skill Builder 2: Buzzword Strategy Match

Purpose

To understand the necessity of using the appropriate buzz-words in business situations.

Instructions

Review each business situation. Note that the best buzzword that fits the situation clearly and effectively has been provided.

Buzzword Strategy Match (15 Examples)

Business Situation	Best Buzzword Choice
Launching a groundbreaking service in a traditional market	Disruptive
Preparing for rapid customer growth	Scalability
Gaining approval for a new internal policy	Buy-In
Building cross-department collaboration on a new project	Synergy
Assigning small, easily achievable tasks early in a project	Low-Hanging Fruit
Encouraging leadership confidence in junior management	Empower
Conducting a complete examination of a supply chain issue	Deep Dive
Quickly checking in with a colleague on project updates	Touch Base
Highlighting the main benefit of a new product in marketing	Value Proposition
Following up after an executive briefing	Circle Back

Business Situation	Best Buzzword Choice
Using existing resources to strengthen a campaign	Leverage
Ensuring open communication about significant changes	Transparency
Inspiring a team to seek creative, innovative ideas	Thought Leadership
Structuring team goals for fast, early successes	Win-Win
Identifying who has time to take on urgent tasks	Bandwidth

Strategic Buzzword Toolkit

CLOSING NOTE

CONGRATULATIONS, YOU HAVE COMPLETED the Strategic Buzzword Toolkit exercises. Every thoughtful step you take to strengthen your communication skills helps you become a clearer, more strategic, and more trusted leader. Remember: Clear language reflects clear thinking. Keep practicing, stay intentional, and let your words work for you.

ABOUT THE AUTHOR

S. Gary Snodgrass is the retired executive vice president and chief human resources officer of a Fortune 100 company. He also served for a decade on the board of a NASDAQ-traded company, where he was lead independent director and chair of major committees.

An accomplished author, Snodgrass has written two previous books—*When Your Career Means Business* and *Stepping Up: 12 Ways to Rev Up, Revitalize, or Renew Your Career*—and is a frequent speaker on business strategy, leadership, career management, and communications. He has led numerous corporate strategy sessions and serves on the adjunct faculty at Trinity College of Jacksonville and Flagler College in St. Augustine, Florida. He holds an MBA and a BS in business administration.

Deeply committed to public leadership and community service, Snodgrass also served two terms as mayor of St. Augustine Beach, Florida. To learn more, visit sgarysnodgrass.com.